Training für mündliche Prüfungen

Englisch Klasse 8–10

Materialien zur Überprüfung von Sprechkompetenz

Cornelsen

Training für mündliche Prüfungen
Materialien zur Überprüfung von Sprechkompetenz, Englisch Klasse 8–10

Redaktion
Chris Caridia, Publishing Services, Berlin

Beratung
Wolfgang Biederstädt, Köln

Layout und technische Umsetzung
sign, Berlin

Grafik
Jeongsook Lee (S. 26, 29, 30, 31, 42, 43, 47, 50, 61)
Christian Bartz (S. 24)
Kathrin Schwertner (S. 25, 27, 28, 59)

Bildquellen
S. 6: K. Berold; S. 8: Comstock; S. 9: Comstock; S. 16 Randy Glasberg; S. 17: Keystone / D. Ecken (fast food restaurant); S. 17: New Zealand Tourism (waiter serving); S. 62: Visum / R. Hackenberg (bear pit); Getty Images / Yellow Dog Productions (campers); S. 64: 10, 11, 12 Randy Glasberg

iStockphoto S. 11: zeynepogan (shopping bags); nano (students and computer); S. 12: huaxiadragon (spectators); 66 blacktiger (messy room); S. 13: bsilvia (man with computer); pryzmat (rubbish); S. 14: mevans (clocks); filo (gorilla); S. 15: seanrmcdermid (rock climber); diego_cervo (sprayer); S. 16: BeholdingEye (laptop); S. 18: tobntno (bride); stask (man by river); S. 19: Nikada (basketball); Cimmerian (jogger); S. 20: Rogeramjet (window cleaner); davelogan (firefighter); S. 21: bradleym (busker); LeggNet (beggar); S. 22: attator (boy on sofa); dwphotos (club); S. 51: StephanHoerold; S. 63: 1 biffspandex (man with guitar); niknikon (hitchhiker); 2 surpasspro (storm damage); jhorrocks (flood) ; 3 sdominik (dog); cynoclub (horse); 4 snapphoto (vets); Anetta R (baby); 5 NinaMalyna (woman with mug); kati1313 (hamburger); 6 ejwhite (parents arguing); jtyler (teen couple); 7 Redemption (UFO); 4201119 (cat); S. 64: 8 Alija (birthday); sharply done (fireworks); JBryson (halloween) 9 stevegeer (houseboat); Topawman (tree house); 10 biffspandex (reading on railway line)

www.cornelsen.de

1. Auflage, 2. Druck 2010

Druck: CS-Druck CornelsenStürtz, Berlin

ISBN 978-3-06-032358-6

Inhalt gedruckt auf säurefreiem Papier aus nachhaltiger Forstwirtschaft.

INHALTSVERZEICHNIS

VORWORT

Stellenwert des Mündlichen
„Sprache" kommt von „sprechen" und nicht von „schreiben". Im Alltag und im Beruf benutzen wir Sprache zu 95% mündlich und nur zu 5% schriftlich.
Eine gute Kommunikationsfähigkeit ist eine Schlüsselkompetenz für das erfolgreiche Meistern aller Lebensbereiche – sei es im späteren Berufsleben oder im privaten Umfeld.

Die prominente Stellung der Mündlichkeit im Fremdsprachenunterricht spiegelt sich in den nationalen Bildungsstandards, dem GER (Gemeinsamer Europäischer Referenzrahmen für Sprachen: lernen, lehren, beurteilen, Berlin 2001) und den jeweiligen Curricula der Bundesländer für das Fach Englisch an allen Schulformen wider. Zunehmend halten daher mündliche Prüfungen in die Profile der Mittleren Schulabschlüsse Einzug, werden mündliche Klassenarbeiten in Form von Präsentationen oder Tandemprüfungen eine Alternative zur schriftlichen Leistungsmessung. Für die Praxis des Englischunterrichts hat diese Stärkung der Mündlichkeit einen positiven *backwash*-Effekt. Schülern und Schülerinnen wird durch die frühe Gewöhnung an mündliche Testsituationen, z.B. durch Interviews, Debatten und Rollenspielen die Angst vor dem freien Sprechen genommen. Der Englischunterricht wird damit seiner Kernaufgabe gerecht, die Lerner zu kompetenten, sach- und adressatengerechten Englischsprechern zu machen.

Zielgruppe und Zielsetzung des Trainingsheftes
Das vorliegende Trainingsheft richtet sich an Schüler und Schülerinnen der Klassen 8–10 (vgl. die entsprechenden Niveaus B1 und B1+ der Mittleren Schulabschlüsse). Es bietet reichhaltiges Übungsmaterial für das Trainieren der Sprechkompetenz mittels unterschiedlicher Aufgabentypen.
Eine mehrteilige mündliche Prüfung oder Klassenarbeit testet alle Bestandteile der Sprechfertigkeit dialogisch (als Partner- oder Gruppenprüfung) sowie monologisch (als Vortrag). Die im Heft enthaltenen Aufgabenformate bilden ein breites Spektrum der einschlägigen Aufgabenformen und Sozialformen (Einzel-, Paar- und Gruppenprüfung) ab. Alle Materialien dieses Heftes sind als Angebot gedacht und können von der Fachlehrerin / dem Fachlehrer den Bedürfnissen der eigenen Lerngruppe angepasst werden.
Zum Beispiel können die Materialien zu Übungszwecken im Unterricht ergänzend zum Lehrwerk verwendet werden. Die Aufgaben sind durch Hilfestellungen angereichert, die den Schülern und Schülerinnen Tipps zum Erwerb von Strategien für das Interagieren in unterschiedlichen Gesprächssituationen geben. *Useful phrases* und Sprachboxen bzw. *Vocabulary Banks* fördern dabei eine systematische Ausweitung des thematischen und strategischen Wortschatzes und verbessern die mündliche Ausdrucksfähigkeit der Lernenden.
Außerdem bietet das Material eine entscheidende Hilfe bei der Vorbereitung und Durchführung von mündlichen Prüfungen, denn die Kopiervorlagen sind unmittelbar einsetzbar.
Am Ende des Heftes befinden sich außerdem zwei Beispiele für mündliche Klassenarbeiten oder Prüfungen inkl. Lösungsschlüssel, in denen verschiedene Aufgabenformen kombiniert werden, sodass unterschiedliche Lerntypen berücksichtigt werden.

Beschreibung der Aufgabenformate
General conversation – Informationsaustausch
Mittels eines Partnerinterviews müssen sich die Schüler und Schülerinnen gegenseitig zu ihrer Person und Biographie befragen. Diese Aufgabe eignet sich gut als „Warming-up" zu Beginn einer Prüfung.

Responding to visual prompts – Zu Bildimpulsen sprechen
Monologisch: Ausgehend von der Beschreibung eines Bildes liefert der Prüfling einen Kommentar oder Interpretation ab, indem er mögliche weitere Details hinzufügt.
Dialogisch: Partner A und Partner B erhalten zwei unterschiedliche Bildimpulse, die sie sich gegenseitig beschreiben müssen, um danach zusammen über ein gemeinsames Thema zu diskutieren.

Simulated Situations – Ausgestalten von Situationen anhand von Bildmaterial
Ausgehend von einem Bildimpuls und der zugehörigen Aufgabe werden die Schüler und Schülerinnen aufgefordert, frei zu assoziieren und über die Situation und ihre Alternativen zu diskutieren sowie Lösungsvorschläge zu erarbeiten. Diese Aufgabe eignet sich auch als Gruppenprüfung (mit drei Schülern).

Role-Plays – Rollenspiele
Bei Rollenspielen erhalten die Beteiligten „role cards“ mit kurzen Beschreibungen der Situation, der beteiligten Personen sowie Stichwörtern. Die Schüler und Schülerinnen versetzen sich in die jeweilige Person und Situation hinein und interagieren miteinander. Hierbei wird die soziale Kompetenz und spontane Sprechfertigkeit trainiert.

Presentations – Referieren und Präsentieren
Die Schüler und Schülerinnen werden durch angeleitete Präsentationen (mit Leitfaden und strukturierenden Sprachmitteln) auf die Prüfungssituation vorbereitet, in der sie freie Vorträge auf Grundlage eines Themenvorschlags halten.

Mediation – Sprachmittlung
Bedeutet im Schulkontext das sukzessive Dolmetschen, d.h. das sinngemäße Übertragen des Gesprächsinhaltes zwischen zwei Personen, die die Sprache des jeweils anderen nicht beherrschen bzw. das Zusammenfassen/Übertragen von Texten in die jeweils andere Sprache (Englisch-Deutsch / Deutsch-Englisch).

Model Tests – Vorlagen für mündliche Prüfungen (inkl. Lösungsschlüssel und Beispiel-Dialogen)
Bietet zwei Beispiele einer mündlichen Prüfung, in der jeweils unterschiedliche Aufgabenformate so kombiniert wurden, dass diese den Anforderungen einer i. d. R. 15-minütigen Tandem-Prüfung entsprechen.

Zu den Inhalten auf der CD-ROM
Enthält editierbare Word-Dateien der Kopiervorlagen, alle Fotos aus den Kopiervorlagen zum Ausdrucken in Farbe, wo diese vorhanden sind, sowie eine Bilddatenbank – *Picture Bank* – mit 25 zusätzlichen Bildern und Fotos.

Tipps für weitere Materialien
Berold, Klaus / Renate Heidemeier. *Go ahead and talk.* 5–10. Cornelsen: Berlin 2009.
Braun, Martin / Christine Wlasak-Feik. *A plus! Die mündliche Prüfung.* Prüfungsaufgaben zu A plus 1–5. Cornelsen: Berlin 2009.
Siebold, Jörg (Hrsg.). *Let's talk. Lehrtechniken.* Vom gebundenen zum freien Sprechen. Cornelsen: Berlin 2006.
Staatsinstitut für Schulqualität und Bildungsforschung München (Hrsg.). *Time to talk.* Eine Handreichung zur Mündlichkeit im Unterricht der modernen Fremdsprachen. Cornelsen: Berlin 2005.
Stevens, John et al. *Listen and Speak. New Edition.* Materialien zur Eurokom. Klasse 10. Cornelsen: Berlin 2008.

A | GENERAL CONVERSATION

What you have to do in this part:
In this part you have to pretend you don't know your partner, and try to find out as much information as possible about him or her by asking and answering questions. You can ask questions about your partner's family, home, school, etc., or talk about likes and dislikes. React to your partner's answers by asking further questions, or by adding to their ideas. Your conversation should be as natural as possible. At one point during the conversation, ask your partner to spell something, for example, his/her name or another difficult word. Talk together for three minutes.

Tips

— Try to be relaxed and confident.

— Speak clearly so that your partner and the examiners can hear you.

— When you answer a question, answer with more than one word.

— Try to give some details. The word 'because' can help you to give reasons.

— Don't forget to smile and look at your partner, not the examiner.

— Remember to use the simple present when you talk about things that you do every day.

— Revise the letters of the alphabet. You will be asked to spell a word in English.

USEFUL PHRASES

Introducing yourself:

Hello, my name's Max Stübinger.
I don't think we've met before. I'm Max Stübinger.

Answering an introduction:

Pleased to meet you.
Hi, Max. **Nice to meet you.**

Asking and answering questions:

Question	Answer
What's your name/first name?	My name is … .
What's your surname/family name?	My surname is … .
Can you spell your surname/family name?	M-U-umlaut-double L-E-R (Müller).
Where/When were you born?	I was born in … in 19… .
Where do you live?	My family and I live in … .
Is it a town or a village?	Well, it's more like a village really, but …
Are there any interesting things to see in … ?	There's an old castle, a museum, … .
Have you got any brothers or sisters?	No, I'm an only child.
What are your hobbies? / What do you do in your spare time?	Well, I really like (…ing). / I'm really into* …
What time do you get up in the morning?	I usually get up at … .
How do you get to school?	In winter I get the bus, but in summer I often cycle or walk.
What are your favourite subjects?	My favourite subjects are … .
What do you think of your English/maths/… teacher?	I think he's absolutely fantastic.
How long have you been learning English?	I've been learning English for about five years.

Showing you're listening:

I've got my own car.
– **Oh, really?** When did you get it?
We live on a boat.
– Oh, do you?
I see. That's interesting!

Giving yourself time to think:

What are your hobbies?
– **Er, let me see.** I really like … .
Is there a museum in Miesbach?
– Yes, **what's it called,**… ?
What's the most recent *Harry Potter* film called?
– The most recent *Harry Potter* film? **Just a minute / hang on a sec*** …
Harry Potter and the Half-Blood Prince, I think.

**Diese Wörter oder Ausdrücke musst du nicht unbedingt lernen.*

NEW FRIENDS

Partner A

Part 1

You've just met your partner. He/She is going to show you a photo of one of the people he/she likes best.

Listen to what your partner tells you and ask at least **12** questions about the person in the photo, for example:

How old is he/she?
Where does he/she live?
Does he/she speak English?
How often do you see him/her?
What does he/she do in his/her spare time?
etc.

Part 2

Now choose one of the photos below and decide whether the person is one of your relatives, a teacher, a friend, etc.

Show the picture to your partner.

Use your imagination to tell your partner as much as you can and answer their questions.
Think about the person's

- name
- age
- family
- hobbies
- interests
- job/school

etc.

Start the conversation by saying to your partner:
Would you like to see a photo of my (English teacher)?

NEW FRIENDS

Partner B

Part 1

You've just met your partner. Choose one of the photos below and decide whether the person is one of your relatives, a teacher, a friend, etc. Show the picture to your partner. Use your imagination to tell your partner as much as you can, and answer their questions.

Think about the person's
- name
- age
- family
- hobbies
- interests
- job/school

etc.

Start the conversation by saying to your partner:
Would you like to see a photo of my (English teacher)?

Part 2

Now your partner is going to show you a photo of one of the people he/she likes best.

Listen to what your partner tells you and ask at least **12** questions, for example:

How old is he/she?
Where does he/she live?
Does he/she speak English?
How often do you see him/her?
What does he/she do in his/her spare time?
etc.

B | RESPONDING TO VISUAL PROMPTS

What you have to do in this part:
In Section 1 you have to describe a picture or photo. You should talk about the things you can see and try to add some personal ideas, e.g. why the people in the picture are where they are, what they are wearing, what the weather is like, how the people in the picture feel, etc. You have to talk about the picture for about one minute.

In Section 2 you will work in pairs. One of you is Partner A, the other Partner B. Each of you has a different picture to describe. First you will talk about your picture as in Section 1. Then your partner will describe his/her picture, while you listen. After this you will talk together and answer a question about the common topic of the two pictures or photos. You should discuss your likes and dislikes. React to your partner's comments by asking further questions. Talk together for about three minutes.

Tips

— Look at your picture or photo carefully and think about what you can say.
— Don't start with details. Make some general comments first. For example: *I think the photo was taken in a classroom/park.*
— Try to mention everything you can see in the picture.
— Use adjectives (*big, small, attractive, young, old*). Don't just name the things you can see.
— If you don't know the word for something in the picture, don't panic. Try to describe it.
— Remember to use the present progressive tense *(is doing)* to describe actions.
— Describe what is going on in the picture, but try to say what is going to happen next as well.

USEFUL PHRASES

Describing photos:

The photo/picture **was taken** in a park/living-room/… .
In the photo/picture **I can see** … .

At the top on the left … .		At the top on the right … .
	In the background there are some … .	
On the left … .	In the centre … . In the middle … .	On the right … .
	In the foreground I can see … .	
At the bottom on the left … .		At the bottom on the right … .

Some people are standing in front of … .
There's a man and he's **…ing**.
I'm not sure, but I think it's a … .
As far as I can see, … .
The weather **looks** good.
It looks like … .

Asking about likes:

Do you like heavy metal?
Are you keen on walk**ing**?
What do you think about … ?
Are you into … ?*

Expressing likes:

I like/love read**ing**.
I'm (not) very keen on swimm**ing**.
I really enjoy in-line skat**ing**.
I'm crazy/mad about* pizza.
I'm (really) into* open-air concerts.

Expressing dislikes:

(I'm afraid) I don't like Chinese food.
I've never liked science fiction films.
I think they are awful/terrible/horrible/boring.

**Diese Wörter oder Ausdrücke musst du nicht unbedingt lernen.*

SECTION 1

B 1.1

Vocabulary Box

- department store
- boutique
- opening hours
- spend
- credit card
- shopaholic
- free time
- material
- quality

1. Describe the photo.
2. What do you think is in the bags?
3. Talk about your shopping habits.
4. Do you ever shop online? What are the advantages and disadvantages?

B 1.2

Vocabulary Box

- humour
- laughter
- funny
- joke
- comedy
- comedian
- relax
- serious
- entertainment
- amusement

1. What can you see in the photo?
2. What do you think the young people are laughing about?
3. Describe some of the things that make you and your friends laugh.
4. 'Laughter is the best medicine.' What do you think this saying means? Do you agree? Give reasons.

B 1.3

Vocabulary Box

- stadium
- spectator
- match
- win
- lose
- shoot
- goal
- miss
- worried
- disappointed
- exciting

1 What does the photo show?

2 What might have happened?

3 Have you ever been to a sports event? Talk about it.

4 Many people watch sports, but not enough people do sports. Do you agree? What about you? Do you do much sport?

B 1.4

Vocabulary Box

- messy
- untidy
- chaos
- lose – lost
- clothes
- tidy up
- space
- hopeless
- share
- angry

1 Describe the room in the photo.

2 Are you a tidy or untidy person? How would you feel if your room looked like this?

3 What do you think the girl's parents say about this room?

4 Describe some situations where there might be a conflict between a tidy and an untidy person.

B 1.5

Vocabulary Box

- environment
- protection
- waste
- rubbish
- global warming
- pollution
- recycle
- re-use
- save
- energy
- electricity

1 What can you see in the picture?

2 Are you optimistic or pessimistic about the future of the planet? Give reasons.

3 What must we do to save our planet?

4 What do you do to help the environment?

B 1.6

Vocabulary Box

- laptop
- crash
- shock
- lose – lost
- data
- important
- terrible
- message
- unexpected

1 How would you describe the moment in the picture?

2 What might have happened?

3 How does the man feel? What will he do/say next?

4 Try to remember a situation where you felt like this. Talk about it.

B 1.7

Vocabulary Box

— hurry
— global
— rush hour
— hectic
— time zone
— speed
— stress
— communication
— modern technology
— slow down
— relax

1 What can you see in the picture?

2 Where do you think the person is going, and why is he in a hurry?

3 Why, in your opinion, is modern life so hectic?

4 In what ways is your life hectic? How could you improve it?

B 1.8

Vocabulary Box

— bars
— cage
— freedom
— shut in
— danger
— die out
— save
— safe
— cruel
— feed – fed

1 What does the photo show?

2 What arguments can you think of for keeping animals in zoos?

3 What arguments can you think of against keeping animals in zoos?

4 Do you like zoos? Why? / Why not?

B 1.9

Vocabulary Box

— extreme
— dangerous
— courage
— courageous
— risk
— adventure
— limits
— challenge
— mountain climbing
— snowboarding

1 What can you see in the photo?

2 Why do people do sports like this?

3 Are people who do extreme sports crazy or courageous?

4 Have you ever tried, or would you ever try, an extreme sport? Why? / Why not?

B 1.10

Vocabulary Box

— graffiti
— spray
— paint
— sprayer
— damage
— cleaning
— expensive
— illegal
— hooligan
— artist
— hood

1 What can you see in the picture?

2 Where can you see graffiti in your town?

3 What kind of people draw or write graffiti? Why do they do it?

4 Some people say that graffiti is an art form and doesn't hurt anybody. What do you think?

B 1.11

Vocabulary Box

- couple
- dating/date
- interests
- in common
- wide choice
- honest
- dishonest
- description
- character
- personality

1. What can you see in the picture?
2. Do you or any of your friends have any experience with online dating?
3. Do you think online dating is a good way to find a partner? Why? / Why not?
4. What are the advantages of online dating? What are the dangers?

B 1.12

"I think he's ready to start using the computer. He just said 'Google'!"

Vocabulary Box

- invention
- invent
- useful
- useless
- depend on
- grow up with
- save time
- convenient
- easy
- progress

1. Talk about the cartoon. What does it tell us about modern life?
2. Imagine life without modern technology. How different would your life be?
3. What do you think was the greatest invention ever? Give reasons.
4. Think of your daily life. What do you really need and what could you live without?

SECTION 2

B 2.1

Partner A

Vocabulary Box
- fast-food
- junk food
- take-away
- cheap
- tasty
- healthy/unhealthy
- meeting place
- outdoors
- relaxed atmosphere

1. Describe to Partner B what you can see on your photograph.
2. Listen to Partner B describing what she/he can see in her/his photograph.
3. Your photographs show people eating in different places. Talk to Partner B about where you enjoy having your meals and about the food you like best. Explain why, and discuss your opinions.

Partner B

Vocabulary Box
- elegant
- service
- tablecloth
- waiter/waitress
- top-quality
- healthy
- expensive
- special occasion
- formal
- stiff

1. Listen to Partner A describing what she/he can see in her/his photograph.
2. Describe to Partner A what you can see on your photograph.
3. Your photographs show people eating in different places. Talk to Partner A about where you enjoy having your meals and about the food you like best. Explain why, and discuss your opinions.

B 2.2

Partner A

Vocabulary Box

- mobile phone
- bride
- wedding
- wedding dress
- veil
- church
- message
- reach
- urgent

1 Describe to Partner B what you can see on your photograph. Who are the people? Where are they? What is the woman wearing? What is she doing?

2 Listen to Partner B describing what she/he can see in her/his photograph.

3 Your photographs show people using mobile phones. Talk to Partner B about the people in your pictures. Who are they talking to? What are they saying? Is the phone call important? What are the advantages and disadvantages of mobile phones? Discuss your opinions.

✂- -

Partner B

Vocabulary Box

- mobile phone
- boat
- rock
- conversation
- message
- on holiday
- reach
- contact
- emergency

1 Listen to Partner A describing what she/he can see in her/his photograph.

2 Describe to Partner A what you can see on your photograph. Where is the young man? What is he wearing? What is he doing?

3 Your photographs show people using mobile phones. Talk to Partner A about the people in your pictures. Who are they talking to? What are they saying? Is the phone call important? What are the advantages and disadvantages? Discuss your opinions.

Partner A

Vocabulary Box

— keep fit
— volleyball
— outdoor(s)
— indoor(s)
— team games
— sporty
— team spirit

1 Describe to Partner B what you can see on your photograph.

2 Listen to Partner B describing what she/he can see in her/his photograph.

3 Your photographs show people doing sports. Talk to Partner B about sports. What do you prefer – team games or individual sports, indoor or outdoor sports? Give reasons. Should there be more sport in schools? Discuss your opinions.

Partner B

Vocabulary Box

— keep fit
— outdoor(s)
— indoor(s)
— fresh air
— exercise

1 Listen to Partner A describing what she/he can see in her/his photograph.

2 Describe to Partner A what you can see on your photograph.

3 Your photographs show people doing sports. Talk to Partner A about sports. What do you prefer – team games or individual sports, indoor or outdoor sports? Give reasons. Should there be more sport in schools? Discuss your opinions.

Partner A

Vocabulary Box

- window cleaner
- office building
- rope
- bucket
- harness
- height
- accident
- earn
- boring
- fear
- dangerous

1 Describe to Partner B what you can see on your photograph.

2 Listen to Partner B describing what she/he can see in her/his photograph.

3 Your photographs show people doing dangerous jobs. Talk to Partner B about these jobs. Which job do you think is more dangerous? Why? Do you think these people earn a lot of money? Is that fair? Talk about a job you would never do and explain why.

Partner B

Vocabulary Box

- firefighter
- danger
- dangerous
- exciting
- fear
- earn
- risk
- accident
- life and death
- injury - injured

1 Listen to Partner A describing what she/he can see in her/his photograph.

2 Describe to Partner A what you can see on your photograph.

3 Your photographs show people doing dangerous jobs. Talk to Partner A about these jobs. Which job do you think is more dangerous? Why? Do you think these people earn a lot of money? Is that fair? Talk about a job you would never do and explain why.

Partner A

Vocabulary Box

- street musician
- earn
- talent
- beg
- beggar
- lazy
- generous
- job/work
- play an instrument
- collect

1 Describe to Partner B what you can see on your photograph.

2 Listen to Partner B describing what she/he can see in her/his photograph.

3 Your photographs show people begging for money on the street. Talk to Partner B about the problems these people have, why they might be where they are, and how you can help them. Do you give them money? Explain why / why not.

Partner B

Vocabulary Box

- beg
- beggar
- lazy
- alcohol
- drugs
- generous
- homeless
- suffer
- hopeless
- charity

1 Listen to Partner A describing what she/he can see in her/his photograph.

2 Describe to Partner A what you can see on your photograph.

3 Your photographs show people begging for money on the street. Talk to Partner A about the problems these people have, why they might be where they are, and how you can help them. Do you give them money? Explain why / why not.

Partner A

Vocabulary Box

— couch potato
— fast food
— take-away
— lazy
— headphones
— unhealthy
— relaxing/relaxed
— lonely
— boring/bored

1 Describe to Partner B what you can see on your photograph.

2 Listen to Partner B describing what she/he can see in her/his photograph.

3 Your photographs show people in their free time. Talk to Partner B about ways of spending your free time. How do you like to spend your free time? Do most people waste their free time? Discuss your opinions.

Partner B

Vocabulary Box

— free time
— dance
— friends
— new people
— noise
— action
— exciting
— interesting

1 Listen to Partner A describing what she/he can see in her/his photograph.

2 Describe to Partner A what you can see on your photograph.

3 Your photographs show people in their free time. Talk to Partner A about ways of spending your free time. How do you like to spend your free time? Do most people waste their free time? Discuss your opinions.

Communication

C | SIMULATED SITUATIONS

What you have to do in this part:
In this part you and your partner have to imagine a situation and talk about it. To give you some ideas for the task, your teacher will give you a piece of paper with pictures on it. You have to reach a decision by discussing the different alternatives. It is important to give your opinion, to make suggestions and to express your feelings. Asking further questions is always a good idea. You should talk together for about four minutes.

Tips

— Don't talk all the time. Give your partner a chance to speak, too. Turn-taking is important.
— Look at all the pictures and say as much as you can about each one.
— Use your imagination. Try to add to your partner's ideas.
— If you don't know a word or phrase, try to find a different way of saying what you want to say.
— Use words such as *maybe*, *perhaps*, etc. if you aren't sure.
— Only come to a decision after you've discussed all the possibilities.

USEFUL PHRASES

Making a suggestion	**Shall we** tell her to go jogging? **What about / How about** join**ing** a tennis club? **Why don't we** advise her to do more sport? **Let's** take the cheapest option.
Asking for someone's opinion	**What do you think/feel about** using the car? **What's your opinion of/view on ...?** **What about** the computer? **Don't you think** ...?
Giving your opinion	**I think** it's a good idea. **In my opinion**, it's great. **If you ask me**, that sounds a bit dangerous. **The way I see it**, it's the only choice.
Asking if someone agrees	**Don't you agree?** **Right? / OK?** **Wouldn't you say so?**
Agreeing	**Yes, I agree.** **That's (quite) true/right.** **That's a great/brilliant idea.** **Exactly.** **You're right.**
Disagreeing	**Sorry, I don't agree.** **I don't think it's a good idea.** **Actually, I think** it's a stupid idea. **You must be kidding!***
Saying you've reached an agreement	**Right, so we agree.** **Well, that's agreed then.** **That's it then.*** **OK then.**

**Diese Wörter oder Ausdrücke musst du nicht unbedingt lernen.*

A weekend in London

Work with a partner. Next weekend you are going to London with your partner, but you can only take one small bag between you. Which **eight** things do you need? Write down your list. Then talk to your partner and write down his or her list. Finally, try to make a list together. Explain to each other why you need the things on your list.

Here are some pictures with some ideas to help you.

What I need:	**What my partner needs:**	**Eight things we will take:**
1 ______	1 ______	1 ______
2 ______	2 ______	2 ______
3 ______	3 ______	3 ______
4 ______	4 ______	4 ______
5 ______	5 ______	5 ______
6 ______	6 ______	6 ______
7 ______	7 ______	7 ______
8 ______	8 ______	8 ______

C **2**

A day with your grandparents

Work with one or two partner(s). Your grandparents are coming to spend the day with you, but your parents are on holiday. Talk together about the things that you could do with your grandparents and then decide how to spend the day. Explain why, and discuss your opinions.

Here are some pictures with some ideas to help you.

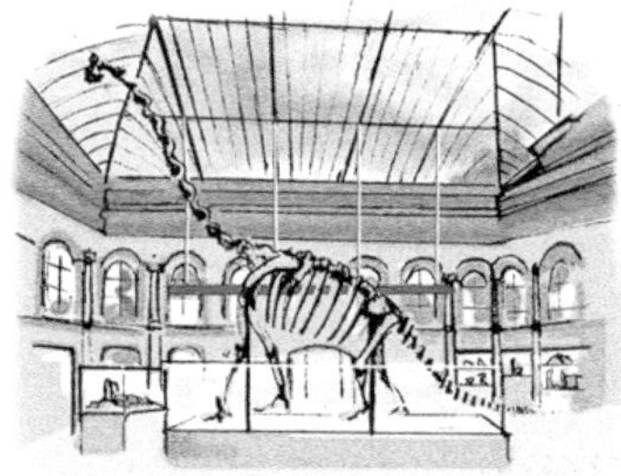

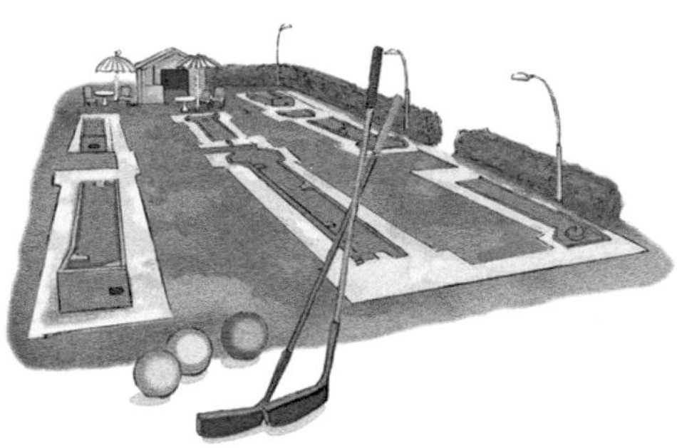

How we will spend the day:

First ______________________________

Then ______________________________

After that ______________________________

____

Little Brother

Work with one or two partner(s). You and your partner(s) are going to take part in a television show called *Little Brother*. You will be locked up in a house together, and will have to stay there for one month. There is food and drink in the house; there is no TV or telephone. Mobile phones are not allowed. There is a computer in the house, but no internet. Together you can take **five** things to help you to pass the time. Decide with your partner(s) which five things to take with you and make a list. Explain to your partner(s) why you would like to take these things.

Here are some pictures to help you.

English-German dictionary

books

English book

computer games

Scrabble

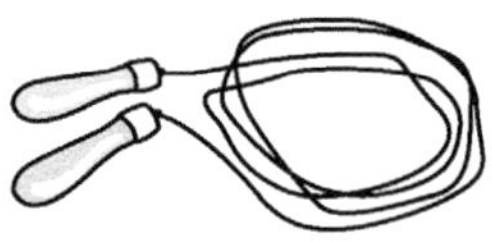

skipping rope

pen and paper

magazines

digital camera

iPod

guitar

exercise bicycle

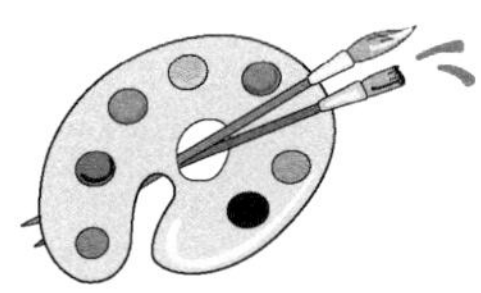

paint brush and paints

Our list:

1 ______________________________

2 ______________________________

3 ______________________________

4 ______________________________

5 ______________________________

C 4

A school celebration

Work with one or two partner(s). Your school will be 50 years old next summer, and you and your teachers want to celebrate. Talk together about the different things you could do and then decide which **three** to choose. Explain why you have chosen these three things and discuss your opinions.

Here are some pictures with some ideas to help you.

Our choice:

1. ______________________________

2. ______________________________

3. ______________________________

C **5**

Decide on a new project

Work with one or two partner(s). Your community has been given a large area of land by a millionaire. The area is going to be used to build different facilities. Talk together about how popular you think these projects would be and then decide which **two** you think should **not** be built. Explain why and discuss your opinions.

Here are some pictures with some ideas to help you.

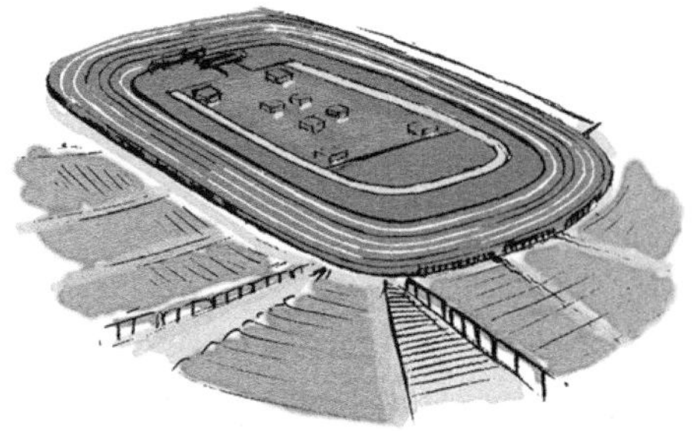

Our choice:

1. ______________________________

2. ______________________________

Class magazine

Work with one or two partner(s). You are going to produce a magazine for your class. You have collected a lot of articles, but the magazine has only six pages and each article is a page long. The readers of the magazine are the same age as you. What will interest them? Which would be the best articles to put in the magazine? Tell each other what you think. Together choose **six** of the articles shown in the pictures below.

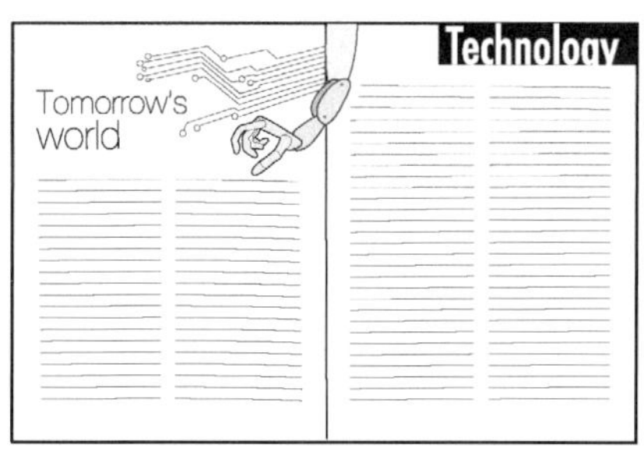

Important inventions

Work with a partner. Your class is working on a project about the most important inventions of all time. You and your partner are going to write about modern inventions. Think of all the important modern inventions you know. Choose **eight** and put them in order of importance (1 = most important). Write your list below. Then write down your partner's list. Finally, try to make a list together.

Here are some pictures to help you.

car

Google
Google

washing machine

mobile phone

computer

light bulb

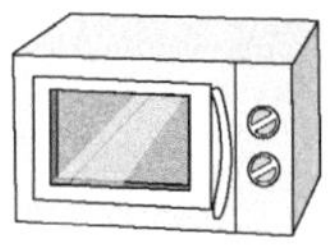
microwave oven

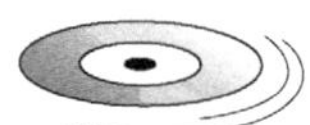
CD

TV

aeroplane

dishwasher

pocket calculator

iPod

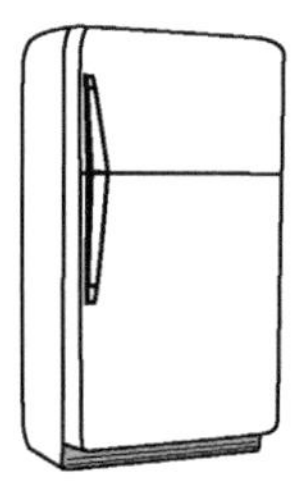
fridge

digital camera

My eight most important inventions:	My partner's eight most important inventions:	Our eight most important inventions:
1 ______	1 ______	1 ______
2 ______	2 ______	2 ______
3 ______	3 ______	3 ______
4 ______	4 ______	4 ______
5 ______	5 ______	5 ______
6 ______	6 ______	6 ______
7 ______	7 ______	7 ______
8 ______	8 ______	8 ______

Planning a holiday

Work with one or two partner(s). You want to go on holiday for three weeks to Australia together. Which parts of Australia would you like to see? How will you travel? What do you want to see and do there? How long will you stay in each place? Remember: Australia is a big country and you only have three weeks. You can't see everything. Here are some pictures with some ideas to help you. Write down your plans in the lines and boxes below.

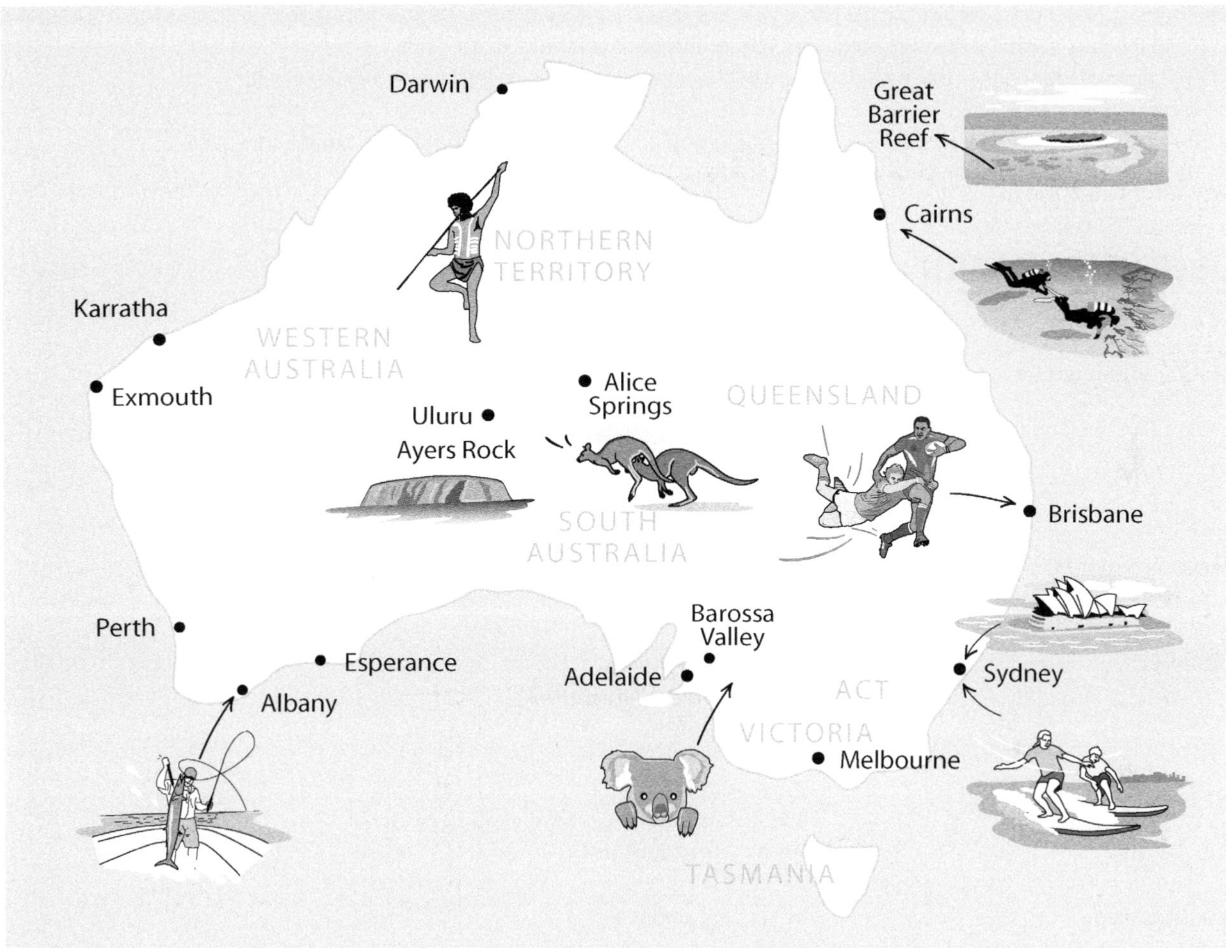

Route:

Transport:

Things to do/see:	**How long?**

D | ROLE-PLAYS

What you have to do in this part:
In this part you and your partner have to imagine a situation and play a role. You will be given a role card that describes the task and gives you some ideas for the role-play. There is some useful vocabulary on the card. It is important to keep the conversation going for three or four minutes.

Tips

— Read the task carefully. Be sure what your role is and what you have to do.
— Try to make your partner talk as much as possible, for example, by asking "open questions" with who/what/when/why/how.
— Try to think how the person (role) you are playing would feel in the situation – angry, happy, nervous? Try to express these feelings.

USEFUL PHRASES

Making first contact	**Good morning, my name is** ... **Excuse me,** ... **I'm sorry,** but ... / **Sorry to bother you,** but ... **Hello, how can I help you?** **I'm phoning about** the advert.
Making requests	**Would you mind** answer**ing** some questions? **I'd really like you to ...**
Agreeing	**You're quite right.** **That's exactly what I think.** **I like that idea.**
Getting angry	**Just a minute ...** **Now, listen to me ... / Now, look here!** **You have no right to ...**
Apologizing	**I'm** terribly **sorry.**
Asking for information	**Could I ask you** a few questions? **Could you tell me ...?** **Do you know if ...?**
Making suggestions	**Why don't we/you** ...? **Do you like the idea of** travell**ing** by train? **How about/What about** tak**ing** a winter break?
Disagreeing	**I don't like that idea.** I'm sorry. **I can't agree.** **I see your point,** but ... **That's nonsense!**
Testing if you understood	**Are you saying** that ...? **Are you trying to tell me** that **...?**
On the phone	**Is that** Mary Smith**?** Mary Smith **speaking.** Mary Smith, Happy Holiday Travel Agency. **How can I help you?**

D 1

☺ Partner A

- You are looking for a job in the evenings, perhaps as a babysitter. You have done this before many times. You have seen an advert in the paper and phone the number.
- You can work any evening except Friday (why not?).
- You can work any week except two weeks in July (why not?).
- You would like to earn £5 an hour before midnight and £7 an hour after midnight.
- You would expect something to eat and a taxi home after midnight.
- Ask for an interview. Address?

Act out your conversation.

Useful words: experience, experienced, reliable, fond of kids

☺ Partner B

- You are looking for a regular babysitter for your two children.
- You put an advert in the newspaper and receive a phone call.
- Say how often you need a babysitter and on which evenings.
- You prefer someone with experience.
- You don't want to pay more than £5 an hour.
- You would take the babysitter home at night.
- Invite for an interview.

Act out your conversation.

Useful words: regular, reliable, prefer, reference

D 2

☺ Partner A

- You are at a restaurant in London together with a friend. Your friend doesn't speak English.
- Ask for the menu and get ready to order the drinks and meals for both of you.
- Ask about the set meal.
- Your friend likes every kind of soup except tomato.
- You would both like a well-done steak.
- You never eat dessert.
- After the meal ask for the bill. You want to pay by credit card.

Act out your conversation.

Useful words: set meal, rare, medium, well-done, starter, main meal, dessert, cash

☺ Partner B

- You work as a waiter/waitress in a London restaurant.
- Two young people come in for lunch. One of them doesn't speak English.
- Ask them if you can take their order.
- The set meal today is:
  - tomato soup
  - steak and chips (steak done how?)
  - chocolate and vanilla ice cream.
- Drinks?
- You don't accept credit cards.

Act out your conversation.

Useful words: set meal, rare, medium, well-done, starter, main dish, dessert, cash

D 3

☺ Partner A

- You are a reporter for the magazine *Cinema*. You are going to interview the film director Steven / Stephanie Playberg, who has just won an Oscar for his/her latest film *The Listener*.
- Introduce yourself.
- Ask him/her when he/she first got the idea for the film, and why he/she wrote it.
- Ask him/her what the film is about.
- Congratulate him/her on winning an Oscar, wish him/her luck for the future, thank him/her for the interview

Act out your conversation.

Useful words: congratulations, plot, stars, award, success, very kind of you

☺ Partner B

- You are the film director Steven/Stephanie Playberg. A reporter from *Cinema* magazine is here to interview you about your latest film *The Listener*, which has won an Oscar.
- Welcome the reporter.
- You read the book many years ago and thought it was wonderful. But you had no money to make the film at that time.
- Tell the reporter what the film is about. (poor man from slums, studies, lawyer, best lawyer in the USA, gets rich, see the film to find out what happens)
- React to the reporter's closing statements.

Act out your conversation.

Useful words: welcome, nice to meet you, plot, broke, successful, award, my pleasure

D 4

☺ Partner A

- You and your friend want to go on holiday together. You would both like to go to New Zealand.
- You would like to camp. It would be an adventure, and it would be cheap.
- You only want to do things you can afford and don't want to take anything from your friend.

Act out your conversation.

Useful words: independent, (can't) afford, proud, outdoors, exciting

☺ Partner B

- You and your friend want to go on holiday together. You would both like to go to New Zealand.
- You would like to stay in a nice hotel, at least for part of the holiday.
- You have got some money from your parents and would be happy to pay for a hotel room for both of you.

Act out your conversation.

Useful words: comfort, luxury, relax, generous, gift

D 5

☺ Partner A

- You work in the office of a ticket agency in New York.
- The phone rings, you answer it. It is a customer.
- Here is some of the information you may need to answer the customer's questions:
  - concert: UKZ
  - place: New York City Town Hall
  - date: 24th January
  - time: 8 p.m. entry 6 p.m.
  - tickets left: 76
  - no seats, only standing-room tickets left
  - price: $39
  - credit cards only
- Finish the conversation.

Act out your conversation.

Useful words: booking, sold out, (no) cash, credit card details

☺ Partner B

- You live in New York. Your favourite progressive rock group is going to play in New York in January.
- Ring the ticket agency and try to get one ticket.
- Details of the concert:
  - band: UKZ
  - place: New York City Town Hall
  - date: 24th January
- You want to know:
  - if there are any tickets left.
  - price? (Your limit is $40.)
  - what time the concert starts.
- How can you pay?
- Reserve a ticket.

Act out your conversation.

Useful words: book, booking, available, cash, credit card

D 6

☺ Partner A

- You are in the London Underground when you see an old friend, who you haven't seen for years.
- You go up to him/her and speak to him/her. He/She is surprised.
- Comment on his/her appearance.
- Ask questions and exchange information:
  - where he/she now lives/works.
  - married, single?
  - contact with other old friends?
  - family?
- Arrange to meet again.

Act out your conversation.

Useful words: ages, (not) changed, move (house), remember, schoolmates, we/you used to …, what happened to …?, what about …?

☺ Partner B

- You are waiting for a train in the London Underground when somebody speaks to you.
- It is an old friend, who you haven't seen for years. You are surprised to see him/her.
- Comment on his/her appearance.
- Ask questions and exchange information:
  - where he/she now lives/works.
  - married/single?
  - contact with other old friends?
  - family?
- Arrange to meet again.

Act out your conversation.

Useful words: ages, (not) changed, move (house), remember, schoolmates, we/you used to … , what happened to …?, what about …?

D 7

☺ Partner A

- You are a policeman or policewoman. You are interviewing a young person about a motorbike accident.
- Ask him/her about …
  - how the accident happened.
  - time and place of the accident.
  - speed.
  - if anyone was injured.
  - his/her protective clothing.
- Check his/her licence and ask him/her to come to the police station later that day.

Act out your conversation.

Useful words: was/were …ing, when it happened, exactly, details, speed limit, injury, helmet, licence, appointment

☺ Partner B

- You have caused an accident with your motorbike.
- A policeman/policewoman asks you some questions.
- Answer the questions.
  - Your motorbike hit a car that came unexpectedly out of a side street.
  - Tell him/her when and where.
- You think you were going too fast, but don't tell the policeman/policewoman.
- Car driver has injuries – what?
- You were wearing a helmet.

Act out your conversation.

Useful words: was/were …ing, when it happened, unexpected, speed limit, slightly injured, seriously injured

D 8

☺ Partner A

- You and your best friend have just finished school. Before you start your apprenticeship, you want to improve your English in a summer language course because you both need it for your future jobs.
- You have checked several brochures and now you want to decide on a course.
- You would prefer to go to England.
  Reasons:
  - accent
  - price
  - 5 lessons a day
  - stay with host families
  - 6 weeks
  - sights

Act out your conversation.

Useful words: description, value for money, accommodation, flight, distance, free-time, tradition

☺ Partner B

- You and your best friend have just finished school. Before you start your apprenticeship, you want to improve your English in a summer language course because you both need it for your future jobs.
- You have checked several brochures and now you want to decide on a course.
- You would prefer to go to the USA.
  Reasons:
  - landscape
  - weather
  - sights
  - 4 lessons a day
  - stay at youth hostel
  - 4 weeks

Act out your conversation.

Useful words: description, accommodation, flight, distance, free-time, adventure, climate

D 9

☺ Partner A

- You are going on holiday with your boyfriend for the first time next month. Last Saturday you went to a party alone and met someone else.
- Now you don't want to go on holiday.
- You know that your girlfriend/boyfriend has made all the arrangements for the holiday.
- You decide to phone him/her and explain why you can't go.

Act out your conversation.

Useful words: regret, apologize, call it off, change my mind

☺ Partner B

- You are going to go on holiday with your boyfriend/girlfriend next month and are really excited. You have made all the arrangements. Almost all the tickets have been bought and the reservations made.
- One evening the phone rings. It is your boyfriend/girlfriend. You are glad he/she has rung, because you want to tell him/her about a very nice and very cheap hotel you have just found.

Act out your conversation.

Useful words: booked, cancel, money back, call it off, change your mind

D 10

☺ Partner A

- You are at the cinema watching a very exciting film. The film is in English and you have to concentrate to understand what is happening.
- Someone next to you is typing text messages on his/her mobile phone. You feel disturbed.
- He/she is also chatting to someone sitting in front of you.
- You can't concentrate on the film and want him/her to stop. You start talking to the person who is disturbing you.

Act out your conversation.

Useful words: disturb, noise, concentrate, difficult, turn off, impolite, apologize

☺ Partner B

- You are at the cinema watching a very exciting film in English. You have seen the film before, so you don't have any problems understanding it.
- You want to meet some friends in town after the film, so you send several text messages and read the answers.
- Another friend of yours is sitting in front of you. You have shown him/her the text messages and spoken in a quiet voice.
- The person next to you starts talking to you.

Act out your conversation.

Useful words: important, necessary, disturb, change seats, apologize

D 11

☺ Partner A

Choose **one** of these topics and tell your partner about it. Listen to his/her problem and try to give him/her some advice.

- Your dad has got a new job and you have to move to another town.
- You saw a friend stealing a mobile phone from a shop.

Act out your conversation.

Useful words: change schools, lose friends, sad, scared, shop assistant, friendship, honesty, lie, discuss, threaten

☺ Partner B

Choose one of these topics and tell your partner about it. Listen to his/her problem and try to give him/her some advice.

- You don't get enough pocket money. Your parents won't give you any more, and they won't allow you to get a job.
- You think your sister is taking drugs, and you don't know what to do.

Act out your conversation.

Useful words: adventure, new friends, chance, friendship, lie, honesty, discuss, threaten

D 12

☺ Partner A

- You are on holiday in Scotland with a friend. You are staying in Edinburgh at the moment, but would like to go to Inverness for a few days.
- Phone the Loch Ness Hotel and make a reservation.
- You need a double room and would like a room with a view.
- Cost of room? Any reduction in price if you stay longer?
- You will arrive by train and want to know if the hotel has a pick-up service.
- You would like an evening meal. Your friend is a vegetarian.

Act out your conversation.

Useful words: view, double room, double bed, single beds, bath, shower, pick-up service

☺ Partner B

- You are a receptionist at the Loch Ness Hotel. Someone phones to book a room.
- You have rooms with a view of the lake available.
- There is a hotel restaurant.
- You need to know:
  - single or double room?
  - with bath or shower?
  - how many nights?
  - dates of arrival/departure.
- The hotel doesn't have a pick-up service, but there are taxis from the station.
- A double room with a view costs £90 per person per night. That includes breakfast.

Act out your conversation.

Useful words: double room, single room, pick-up service, price reduction

D 13

☺ Partner A

- You have been on holiday in Malaysia and have fallen in love with a boy/girl from that country. You are very, very happy.
- Describe the boy/girl.
- You have decided you want to give up your life in your home country, buy a beach house in Malaysia, and live there with him/her for ever.
- Tell your friend about your decision.

Act out your conversation.

Useful words: dream, future, idyllic, romantic, true love, certain, for life, chance of a lifetime

☺ Partner B

- Your friend tells you about a decision he/she has made. Listen carefully and then react.
- You think your friend has gone mad and has made a terrible decision.
- Think of all the reasons why your friend's plan is crazy.
- Try to convince him/her not to do it.

Act out your conversation.

Useful words: dream, nightmare, sense, sensible, (not) last, stranger, ruin your future

D 14

☺ Partner A

- You've just started working for a company in Leeds. Last month you found a two-bedroom flat. It's rather expensive (£800 a month).
- You are looking for someone to share the flat with you.
- You hate smoking and drinking alcohol.
- You have to get up very early in the mornings.
- You have got a cat.
- You want somebody to share the rent and all household jobs.

The doorbell rings and you open the door.

Act out your conversation.

Useful words: hate … -ing, (don't) mind … -ing, dislike … -ing, expensive, prefer, rent, share, cleaning

☺ Partner B

- You are looking for a flat or room in Leeds. Yesterday you read an advert offering a room in a two-bedroom flat.
- You don't want to pay more than £400 a month.
- You don't mind doing jobs in the house.
- You don't like animals very much.
- You smoke, but you don't drink alcohol.
- You should ask about:
  - the rent.
  - using the kitchen.
  - smoking in your room.
  - animals.
  - guests allowed?

You have gone to the flat to see the room.
Ring the doorbell.

Act out your conversation.

Useful words: (don't) mind … -ing, dislike … -ing, expensive, prefer, rent, share, cleaning

D 15

☺ Partner A

- You are walking in the park when you notice a well-dressed person stand up from a bench and walk away, leaving an empty sandwich paper, a cardboard coffee cup and a newspaper behind on the bench. There is a rubbish bin nearby.
- You are a very environment-friendly person and hate to see such pollution.
- You stop the person and start a polite conversation.
- Try to make the person take the rubbish to the bin.

Act out your conversation.

Useful words: cardboard cup, rubbish bin, waste, pollution, environment, responsible, global warming

☺ Partner B

- You work in an office and have just had your take-away lunch on a bench in the park.
- You suddenly realize that it is late and you have to hurry back to work.
- You leave your sandwich paper and empty cardboard coffee cup on the bench.
- There is already an old newspaper lying there.
- Somebody stops you and speaks to you.

Act out your conversation.

Useful words: cardboard cup, rubbish bin, waste, pollution, environment, responsible, factories, cars

D 16

☺ Partner A

- You are the parent of a five-year old child.
- You and your wife are going on holiday for three weeks and your child will stay with her grandparents (your parents).
- Your problem is that your parents spoil[1] the child.
- Before you go on holiday, you have to discuss with them:
  - giving the child sweets
  - not making the child eat up her vegetables
  - letting the child stay up late
  - too much TV
  - buying her whatever she wants
  - etc.

Act out your conversation.

[1]spoil *verwöhnen*

Useful words: teeth, weight, healthy diet, TV programme, (un-)suitable, fresh air and exercise

☺ Partner B

- You are the grandmother/grandfather of a five-year old child. Your son/daughter and his wife/her husband are going on holiday, and your grandchild will stay with you for three weeks.
- You believe that the role of parents is to discipline their children, and the role of grandparents is to spoil[1] them. For example, you believe:
  - children should be allowed to eat what they like.
  - TV helps a child's imagination.
  - children have a lot of energy and fall asleep when they are ready.
- Your son/daughter wants to speak to you before they leave. Listen to what he/she says and reply.

Act out your conversation.

[1]spoil *verwöhnen*

Useful words: healthy diet, weight, pleasure, (un-)suitable, TV programme

E | PRESENTATIONS

What you have to do in this part:
In this part you have to prepare and give a presentation. You should talk for about four minutes.

How to give a successful presentation

Step 1: Choose your topic
Choose something that you are interested in. For example, you can talk about one of your hobbies, or a person or place that really interests you. Remember, you have only a few minutes to talk, so try to make it interesting for your listeners. Prepare to answer your listeners' questions.

Step 2: Research your topic
You can use different media to help you find information on your topic: books, magazines, encyclopaedias, the internet, etc. Two online encyclopaedias that you might find useful are: *www.infoplease.com* and *www.encyclopedia.com.*

Step 3: Prepare your talk
Decide what you want your audience to know when you have finished your talk. Use only material that will help them to understand that information. You can use a mindmap (see page 43) to brainstorm and collect your ideas, then write the main points you want to make on separate note cards. Write clearly in English. Note down keywords and useful phrases. Only write down the important things. Put your note cards in order and number them.
How can you make your talk more interesting? Think of visuals (see Step 5), jokes, sounds.

Step 4: Practise your talk
Practise your presentation at home. Try it alone first, perhaps in front of a mirror, or using a webcam or camcorder. Then try it in front of other people: your parents, a friend. Keep an eye on the time.

Step 5: Use visuals
Visuals make a presentation more interesting and can help your audience to remember important points. But be careful – too many visuals will distract your listeners. You can use:
- pictures that illustrate your points,
- objects that the listeners can look at,
- the board or overhead projector to show graphs, diagrams or tables, or a summary of your main points.

Step 6: Give your presentation
- Before you start, take a deep breath.
- Stand up straight. If you need to, walk around a bit.
- Introduce your topic.
- Explain the structure of your talk.
- Speak slowly and clearly, and look at your listeners while you speak.
- Look at your audience, not at your notes. Only use your notes as reminders.
- Explain difficult words and tell your listeners when you are moving on to a new point.
- Make a brief summary at the end of your talk.
- Find a good finishing sentence.
- Thank your listeners and ask them if they have any questions.

---

visuals *pictures, photographs, graphs*
distract *ablenken*
object *Gegenstand*

Tips

- Try to relax and enjoy your talk. If you do, your listeners probably will, too.
- Prepare your presentation well. Make clear notes in English.
- Speak loudly and clearly. Don't talk too fast.
- Keep things simple and clear for your audience.
- Make eye contact with your listeners.
- Visuals will make your presentation more interesting.
- Give lots of examples.
- Keep an eye on the time.

USEFUL PHRASES

Introduction	**My name** is ... and **I would like to talk about** … **I've chosen this topic because** …
Structure	**I would like to divide my talk into** … parts … **In the first part, I will** … **First** …, **then** …, **after that** … . **Finally** … **Next** I would like to take a look at … **My next point** is about …
Giving examples	**As an example** … / **For example**, … **Let me give you** one/a couple of **example(s)**.
Explaining	**That means** … **Let me explain** in more detail / that again. **Generally speaking** …
Using visuals	**Here you can see** … **The next picture shows** …
Finishing	**I'd like to finish** by summarizing … **That brings me to the end of my presentation.** **Thank you for listening.**
Question time	**Are there any questions?** **I would be happy to answer any questions.** **I'm not quite sure I understood** your question. **I'm afraid I don't know exactly, but I can find out.**

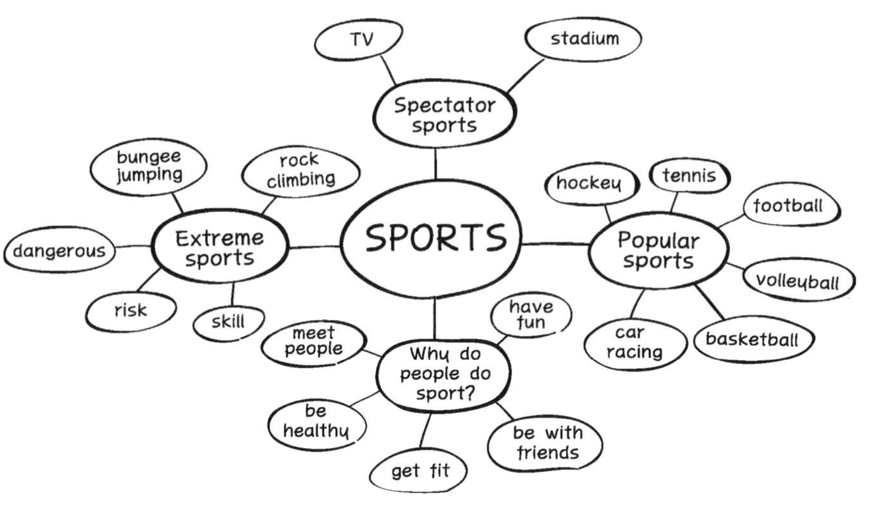

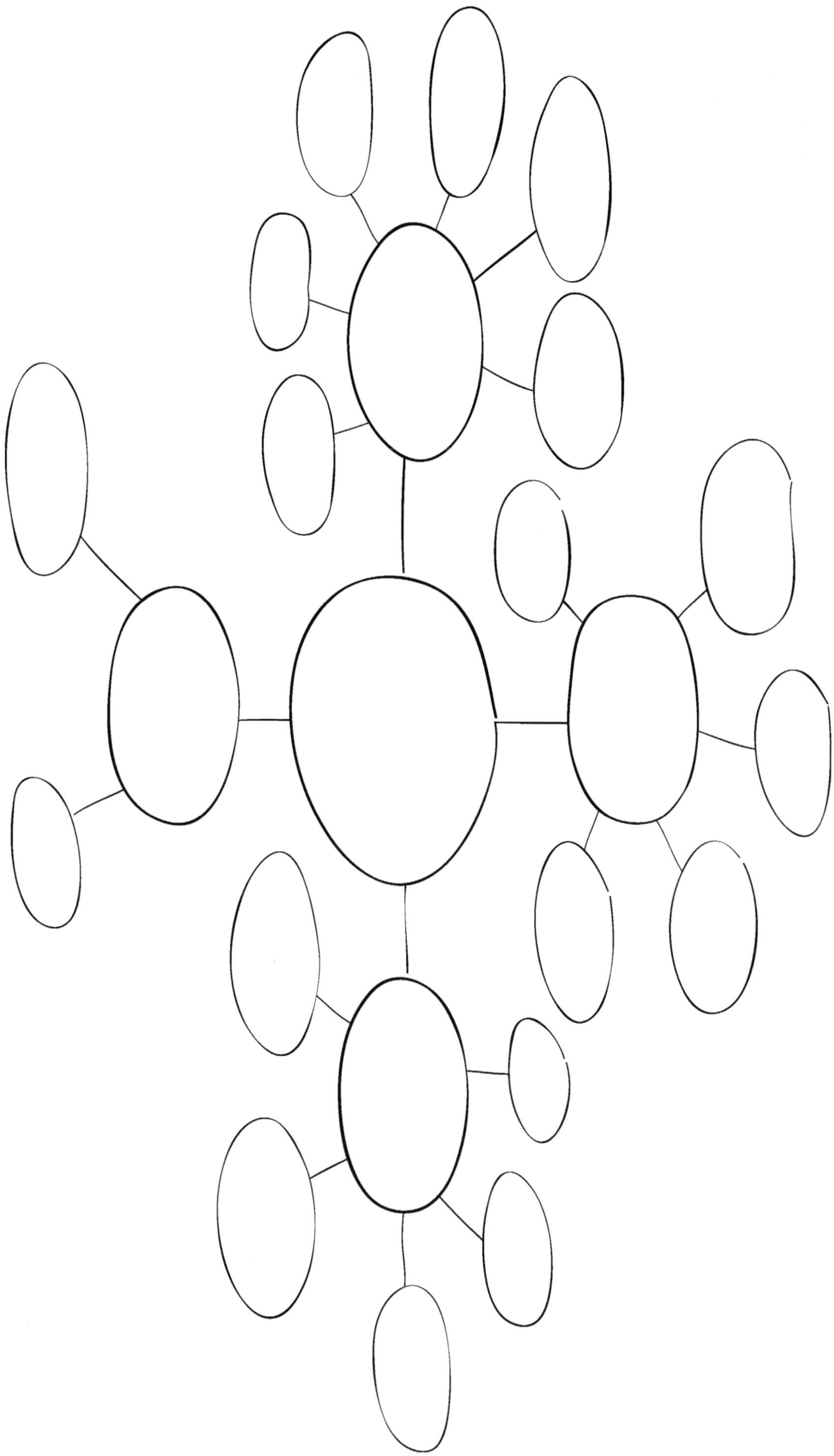

SECTION 1: Guided presentations

E 1.1

Match the phrases with the functions. The first one has been done for you.

Function	Phrase
1 Introduction	a I would be happy to answer any questions.
2 Structuring	b … some of the stamps I have brought with me today.
3 Giving examples	c … brings me to the end of my presentation.
4 Explaining	d Today I would like to talk about …
5 Using visuals	e First of all … .
6 Finishing	f Let me give you a couple of examples.
7 Question time	g I would like to explain …

E 1.2

Now put the phrases from E1.1into the gaps in the short presentation below.

Hello, my name is Ted. ______________________________ my favourite hobby – collecting stamps. ______________________________ I would like to tell you how I started this hobby. Then I'll show you ______________________________.

I started this hobby when I was eight years old, and my uncle gave me the stamp collection he had when he was a boy.

There are a lot of different ways of finding interesting stamps. ______________________________ ______________________________. One way is to have pen friends who live in other countries. I have two – one in Japan and one in Canada. Another way is to join a stamp collectors' club, either online or in the town where you live. You can also get stamps on e-bay.

If you get stamps on letters or parcels, you have to remove them. ______________________________ the best way to do that: put the stamp face down in warm water. Leave it for a few moments, and then it is easy to take it off the paper. Dry it with paper towels.

Now I would like to show you some of my best stamps. This one is from Japan. It's not very valuable, but it's very pretty, don't you agree? The next one is …

…

That was the last stamp I wanted to show you and it ______________________________.
Thank you for listening.

And now ______________________________

E 1.3

Prepare a presentation about your favourite TV programme. Use the sentences below to help you.

Hello, my name is …
I would like to talk about my favourite TV programme, which is …
It is on at … (*time*) on … (*day*).
I always watch it live. / I usually record it.
I usually watch the programme alone/with my mum/with a friend.
It's a soap opera/comedy/thriller/documentary/ …
It's about …
My favourite character is … .He/She is played by …
I like … because …
Let me tell you what happened in the last episode/show.

E 1.4

Talk about your family. The words in the boxes can help you. Perhaps you have some photos or other things, too.

I have — a mother — a stepmother — a father — a stepfather — … brother(s) — … sister(s) My … also live(s) with us.	I'm older/younger than … My brother/My sister is … I'm the oldest/youngest child in the family. My … is/are …. years old.	We have a dog/cat/hamster/rabbit/… We don't have any pets/animals.	We live in a house/flat. We live in the town/ country. I have my own room. / I share a room with … We have/don't have a garden/balcony. Our house/flat is near our school/the shops.

SECTION 2: Free presentations

Prepare and give a 4-minute presentation on one of the following topics:

1	My favourite hobby
2	My family
3	A summer holiday
4	My pet
5	My best friend
6	A famous person
7	A historical person
8	The country/city that interests me most
9	My favourite sport
10	My town/city
11	An important event in my life
12	Saving the environment
13	A healthy life
14	Life in the future

F | MEDIATION

What you have to do in this part:
In Section 1 you will be given prompts in English and you have to pass on the information to someone in German. In Section 2 the prompts are in German and you have to pass on the information in English. In Section 3 you have to use English and German to help two other people to communicate.

Tips
- It is not necessary to translate word-for-word. You only need to pass on the most important information in your own words.
- Don't only think about what you have to say. Listen carefully to what your partner says so that you can react.
- If you don't know a word, don't panic. Use your own words to get the meaning across.

SECTION 1: English to German

F 1.1

Signs

You are in Great Britain with a German friend who doesn't speak English. You see the signs below. Explain to your friend in German what the signs mean.

F 1.2

A message

Your American pen friend, Cathy, has left the message below on your answerphone. Your mother doesn't understand English, and she would like to know what Cathy said. Tell your mother in German what your pen friend said.

"Hi, this is Cathy. I'm calling today to wish you and the family Happy Thanksgiving. I know you don't celebrate that in Germany, but I wanted to send you my best wishes all the same. My family and I are going to have a big turkey dinner this evening. I will send you an email and tell you how Thanksgiving started. It's really interesting.
But for now, just say 'Hi' to everyone for me. Bye."

F 1.3

A film review

You have read this review in English of the film *Benjamin Button* and would like to tell your parents what the film is about in German. Make notes in German of the information you would like to give them.

The strange story is told by Daisy (Cate Blanchett), who is dying in a New Orleans hospital, as Hurricane Katrina approaches in August 2005. She asks her daughter, Caroline, to read to her from her diary about the love of her life, a man named Benjamin Button (Brad Pitt). He was born in 1918. He was over eighty years old when he was born and lived his life backwards, getting younger as time passed. We follow the story, set in New Orleans, from the end of World War I into the 21st century. It is a story of an unusual man and the people and places he discovers, the love he finds, the pleasures of life and the sadness of death.

Bullying

You have found the following information about bullying on the internet. You would like to tell your parents about it. Write down the main facts in German.

What is bullying?
Bullying is aggressive behaviour by one individual or a group to frighten someone, exclude them from group activities, or damage their things.

What can I do if my child is being bullied?
A child might not tell his or her parents about bullying because the child often feels ashamed. Look out for signs. Does your child often have stomach aches or headaches? Does he or she sleep badly, or have nightmares? Is he or she nervous about going to school?

If your child wants to talk to you about bullying, listen and try to give support. It is hard for a victim to do anything to stop the problem, so it is important to offer help. Ask your child how he or she has dealt with the bullying so far and make further suggestions. Tell your child to ignore the bully and walk away. It is important to tell a teacher whenever bullying happens, or at least to inform an adult. Your child should always have the telephone numbers of people he or she trusts.

Take action yourself – but only if your child agrees. Discuss the bullying with other parents; go to the school to speak to the teachers.

New York

You are on holiday with your parents in New York. You have got some information about places to see. Your parents don't understand English very well. Tell them the most important pieces of information in German to help them decide what they would like to see.

- It's no longer the world's tallest skyscraper, but the 102-storey **Empire State Building** on Fifth Avenue is a popular place for visitors to the city. It was opened in 1931 after only 410 days of building. The building is 1,472 feet high and has an outside observation deck on the 86th floor. On a clear day you can see for almost 80 miles. The observation deck[1] is open seven days a week from 9.30 a.m. to midnight. Nearest subway stations to the Empire State Building: 33rd Street or 34th Street, subway line 6.

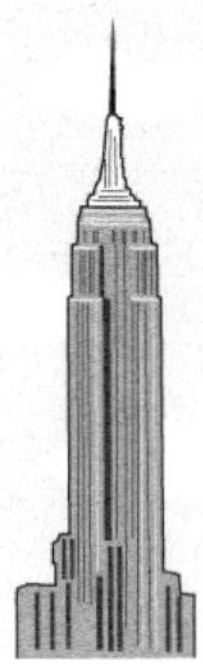

[1]observation deck *Aussichtsplattform*

- **Ellis Island**
Between 1892 and 1954, 12 million immigrants entered the United States from this island in New York Harbor. They were greeted by the Statue of Liberty, which stands nearby.

With films, archives, photos and recordings, the Ellis Island Immigrant Museum shows visitors what happened when immigrants arrived in America. Some were allowed in, others were sent home, some died in the hospital here.

Ticket price is included in the ferry fare. Ferry leaves from Battery Park every half hour. Tickets: adults $12, children under 14 $6.

- **Central Park** is in the middle of Manhattan Island. It runs two and a half miles from 59th Street to 110th Street and half a mile from Fifth Avenue to Eighth Avenue. It was one of the first city parks in the United States. The idea for the park began in the early 1850s. The project took more than ten years to finish and cost the city ten million dollars. Today the park has many good restaurants. You can take a boat trip on one of the lakes and, of course, you can also visit the famous Central Park Zoo.

- **The Statue of Liberty** in New York Harbor has welcomed millions of immigrants who have come to America to start a new life. It was a gift to America from France in 1886 to celebrate the Declaration of Independence on 4th July, 1776. To visit the statue, take a ferry from Battery Park. The trip takes 15 minutes. Ferries run seven days a week from 8.30 a.m. to 4.30 p.m. You can enter the statue, and after that relax and have a picnic on Liberty Island.

SECTION 2: German to English

F **2.1**

A holiday in Germany

Your Irish friend Tim from Dublin is visiting you. His family are planning to go on holiday to the Rhineland next summer and he has got a brochure about the River Rhine. Tim doesn't understand all the German. Read the brochure and answer his questions.

Urlaub am Rhein – einer der größten und schönsten Flüsse Europas. Kilometerlang erstrecken sich Radwege entlang des Flusses. Machen Sie eine schöne Schifffahrt nach Koblenz oder zur berühmten Loreley. Besuchen Sie einige wunderschöne Rheinschlösser – jedes mit seiner eigenen erstaunlichen Geschichte.

Das Hotel Kastanienhof liegt in dem kleinen Ort Bacharach am Rhein. Das Hotel hat 20 Zimmer und befindet sich nur zehn Gehminuten vom Ortskern entfernt.

Alle Zimmer sind bequem eingerichtet und verfügen über Dusche/WC und Fernseher. Täglich wird ein Frühstücksbuffet angeboten. Im Hotel befinden sich ein Aufenthaltsraum und ein Fahrradraum. Sie können bei uns Räder von bester Qualität mieten[1].

Preise: Übernachtung mit Frühstück ab 30 Euro pro Person.

1 Is it a good place to go cycling?

____

2 Where can we rent a bike?

____

3 What other activities can we do?

____

4 What does the hotel offer?

____

5 What are the rooms like?

____

6 What does bed and breakfast normally cost?

____

[1]mieten *rent*

F 2.2

An email from Germany

You are in Australia on an exchange visit. Your parents have sent you an email with some messages for you to pass on to your host family. What would you say to your host family in English?

Subject:

… und bedanke dich bitte bei deiner Gastfamilie, besonders der Mutter und dem Vater, dass du bei ihnen einen Monat wohnen kannst. Du sollst ihnen auch für die Fotos von ihrem Haus und der Stadt danken, die sie uns geschickt haben. Der Swimmingpool ist wunderschön. Wir würden gern auch einen Pool in unserem Garten haben, aber das Wetter hier ist nicht so warm wie in Australien.
Sag ihnen auch, dass wir uns sehr darauf freuen, dass die Familie nächstes Jahr nach Deutschland kommt.
Wir haben viel geplant und werden mit ihnen eine Reise durch Deutschland machen.
Schöne Grüße auch an die Kinder.
Tschüß
Deine Mama

F 2.3

Anti-ex programme

Your Australian friend has sent you an email. He is really depressed because his girlfriend has finished with him. You saw this 'anti-ex programme' in a German magazine. You think it might help your friend. He doesn't speak German, so you will have to write down the most important information in English.

Wie kann ich meinen Ex endlich vergessen? Tipps, wie du wieder glücklich wirst!
Egal, ob du Schluss gemacht hast oder er/sie: es tut weh. Und wenn er/sie dir nicht mehr aus dem Kopf geht, hast du ein Problem. Wie kannst du ihn/sie endlich vergessen? Hier ein paar Tipps:

1 Pack alle Fotos und Erinnerungsstücke weg und lass sie im Keller – zumindest für ein paar Monate. Lösche alle Emails.
2 Spar dir die „Können-wir-nicht-Freunde-bleiben?"-Nummer! Das geht nicht gut.
3 Frag nicht nach der/dem Neuen. Das willst du wirklich nicht wissen.
4 Schreib ihm/ihr einen Abschiedsbrief. Den Brief sollst du dann verbrennen oder in kleine Stücke reißen und wegschmeißen. Das hilft und macht den Kopf wieder klar.
6 Mach Sport oder geh tanzen. Die Bewegung tut dir gut und du fühlst dich wohler.
7 Geh wieder aus. Flirt mal wieder – nur zum Spaß. Bald geht es dir besser.

Tokio Hotel

Your English pen friend has heard about the German band Tokio Hotel and asks you in an email for more information about them. You have found the text below on the internet. Write and tell your friend the most important pieces of information. You can write about:

- who does what in the band.
- when, where and how the band was formed.
- their first video and first album.
- their success abroad.

TOKIO HOTEL

Gründung: 2001
Genre: Pop/Rock (deutsch)
Website: http://www.tokiohotel.de

Mitglieder: Bill Kaulitz (Gesang)
Tom Kaulitz (Gitarre)
Georg Listing (Bass)
Gustav Schäfer (Schlagzeug)

Gründung

Die Zwillinge Bill und Tom Kaulitz (geb. 1. September 1989) machen seit ihrer Kindheit zusammen Musik. Bei einem Auftritt im Jahr 2001 in ihrer Heimatstadt Magdeburg trafen sie Gustav Schäfer (geb. 8. September 1988) und Georg Listing (geb. 31. März 1987), mit denen sie die Band *Devilish* gründeten. Die Band wurde im Jahr 2003 vom Musikproduzenten Peter Hoffmann entdeckt und änderte ihren Namen in *Tokio Hotel*. 2005 nahm die Universal Music Group die Band unter Vertrag und erarbeitete einen umfangreichen Marketingplan, um den kommerziellen Erfolg der Band zu sichern.

Debüt

Das Video zu ihrer Debütsingle *Durch den Monsun* wurde im Juli 2005 im Fernsehen ausgestrahlt. Das Ende September 2005 veröffentlichte Debütalbum *Schrei* stieg an die Spitze der Charts in Deutschland und Österreich.

Erfolge im Ausland

Als eine der wenigen deutschen Bands ist *Tokio Hotel* auch im fremdsprachigen Ausland erfolgreich. *Tokio Hotel* ist die erste deutsche Band, die mit einem Debüt-Album in die französischen Top 20 gelandet ist.
Im November 2006 spielte die Band ein Konzert in Moskau vor mehreren tausend Besuchern. 2008 fanden Konzerte in sieben Ländern statt und *Scream* wurde in Großbritannien und anderen europäischen Ländern veröffentlicht[1].

[1] veröffentlicht *released*

SECTION 3: German to English and English to German

F	3.1

A guest from New Zealand

Your pen friend, Cathy, is from New Zealand. She is staying with you and your family. She doesn't speak German. Your friend Timo has invited you both to his house and he would like to know what Cathy likes to eat. He doesn't speak much English, so you have to help them.

TIMO Was möchte Cathy heute Abend essen?

YOU (to Cathy) ______________________________

CATHY What do you usually have?

YOU (to Timo) ______________________________

TIMO Wir essen meistens kalt – Brot, Käse, Obst.

YOU (to Cathy) ______________________________

CATHY That sounds fine.

YOU (to Timo) ______________________________

TIMO Gut. Was möchte sie trinken?

YOU (to Cathy) ______________________________

CATHY Juice, please.

YOU (to Timo) ______________________________

TIMO Was für Saft? Wir haben Apfelsaft oder Orangensaft.

YOU (to Cathy) ______________________________

CATHY Apple juice, please. And could I have some mineral water, too?

YOU (to Timo) ______________________________

TIMO Kein Problem. Hat sie jetzt schon Hunger oder sollen wir später essen?

YOU (to Cathy) ______________________________

CATHY I'm hungry. If it's okay with you, I'd like to eat now, please.

YOU (to Timo) ______________________________

At the doctor's

Your Australian friend, Craig, is visiting you. He can't speak German. He doesn't feel well, so you go with him to a German doctor. Unfortunately the doctor doesn't speak English, so you have to help them.

CRAIG Tell him I have stomach ache, please.

YOU (to the doctor) ______________________________

DOCTOR Hat er auch Kopfschmerzen?

YOU (to Craig) ______________________________

CRAIG No, I haven't. But I feel very tired.

YOU (to the doctor) ______________________________

DOCTOR Hat er etwas Ungewöhnliches gegessen?

YOU (to Craig) ______________________________

CRAIG Not really. But your German food is very different for me. And your bread is much heavier than ours. Perhaps I've eaten too much of it.

YOU (to the doctor) ______________________________

____

DOCTOR Er soll heute nichts mehr essen. Nur Tee trinken und sich ausruhen. Wenn es ihm Morgen nicht besser geht, kommen Sie mal wieder.

YOU (to Craig) ______________________________

____

CRAIG Tell him, thanks. I hope I don't have to come back again tomorrow.

YOU (to the doctor) ______________________________

A souvenir

Your friend Jim from Ireland is visiting you. He wants to buy a souvenir to take home for his mother. Jim doesn't speak German. You have to help him.

JIM	Tell her I don't want to spend more than 30 euros.
YOU (to shop assistant)	
SHOP ASSISTANT	Mag seine Mutter Süßigkeiten?
YOU (to Jim)	
JIM	Well, she does. But she's trying to lose weight.
YOU (to shop assistant)	
SHOP ASSISTANT	Verstehe. Wie wäre es mit einer CD mit deutscher Musik?
YOU (to Jim)	
JIM	Sorry. Mum only likes Irish folk music.
YOU (to shop assistant)	
SHOP ASSISTANT	Ich habe eine andere Idee. Wie wäre es mit einem schönen Buch mit Bildern von Deutschland?
YOU (to Jim)	
JIM	But Mum can't read German.
YOU (to shop assistant)	
SHOP ASSISTANT	Das ist kein Problem. Wir haben auch Bücher auf Englisch.
YOU (to Jim)	
JIM	What do they cost?
YOU (to shop assistant)	
SHOP ASSISTANT	Die Preise fangen bei 15 Euro an.
YOU (to Jim)	
JIM	Could she show me one for 25 euros, please?
YOU (to shop assistant)	

TEST ONE

General conversation

Examiner: I'd like you to pretend that you don't know each other. Ask questions to find out as much information as possible about each other.

Role play

☺ Partner A

- You are the parent of a teenage son/daughter.
- Your son/daughter is going out with somebody you don't like.
- You saw this boyfriend/girlfriend yesterday in a café with another girl/boy. They were kissing. You are not sure if your son/daughter knows.
- Your son/daughter seems rather unhappy lately.
- Speak to your son/daughter about his/her feelings.

Act out your conversation.

☺ Partner B

- You have been going out with a boy/girl for two months.
- You know your parents don't like your boyfriend/girlfriend.
- You are not sure about your boyfriend/girlfriend yourself and have heard rumours[1] that he/she has been seeing somebody else.
- You want to live your own life and don't want your parents telling you what to do, or asking a lot of questions.
- Your mum/dad asks you how you are feeling.

Act out your conversation.

[1]rumour *Gerücht*

Mediation English-German

Tips for a walking tour

You are planning a walking trip in Scotland with some German friends. You have found the tips below on the internet. Write down the most important information in German to tell your friends. You should mention the following:

1 weather
2 equipment
3 planning
4 food and drink
5 emergencies

Tips for walking

— Check the weather forecast before you leave. It is also a good idea to have an alternative route planned in case the weather is worse than forecast.

— A basic minimum of equipment to take on the hills is: waterproofs[1], map, compass and torch[2]. Check and pack your things the day before you leave.

— Know your route. Check with guidebooks, magazines, friends and on the web to find out what sort of countryside (e.g. flat, hilly, etc) you will cross.

— Take time to plan and prepare for your trip. Always plan around the ability of the weakest member in a group.

— It is not easy to find enough to drink in the countryside, so take enough with you. Take high-energy foods such as chocolate, banana chips, dried fruit and nuts. A flask with hot soup or a hot drink will be very welcome on a cold, wet day.

— Eating 'little but often' is my personal top tip for hill-walking. Carry some sweets in your pockets as these will give you energy.

— Always take your mobile phone with you (in a waterproof bag). In an emergency it will save valuable time if you can get help quickly.

[1]waterproofs *wasserdichte Kleidung*
[2]torch *Taschenlampe*

Simulated Situation

Meeting people

Work with one or two partner(s). Your Aunt Betty, who is 53, is lonely. She wants to find a new spare time activity where she can get fit and meet other people. Decide which activity would be best for her and talk about where in your area she could do it. Explain why you have chosen that activity and discuss your opinions.

Here are some pictures with some ideas to help you.

We think the best activity for Aunt Betty would be ______________________________

because ______________________________

____

____

____

TEST TWO

General conversation

Examiner: I'd like you to pretend that you don't know each other. Ask questions to find out as much information as possible about each other.

Mediation German-English

Writing a CV

Your English friend has to write a CV and has asked you in an email if you have any idea how to do it. You have found a website in German with some useful tips. Your English friend doesn't understand much German. Write down the main ideas in English to send to her.

Lebenslauf

Ihr Lebenslauf soll alle wichtigen Fakten enthalten. Er muss übersichtlich[1] und leicht zu lesen sein. Sie können Ihren Lebenslauf als Tabelle schreiben, entweder in der zeitlichen Reihenfolge („chronologisch“) oder beginnend mit der jetzigen Situation („amerikanisch“).
Er muss folgende Informationen enthalten:

- **Persönliche Daten:** Das sind Ihr Name und Ihre Anschrift, Ihr Geburtsdatum und -ort sowie Ihr Familienstand[2].
- **Ausbildung:** Sie können mit der Grundschulzeit beginnen. Schulabschluss mit Note sollte erwähnt werden.
- **Berufliche Praxis:** Nennen Sie alle bisherigen Tätigkeiten mit kurzer Darstellung der wichtigsten Aufgaben. Geben Sie auch Praktika, Nebenjobs oder sonstige Tätigkeiten an.
- **Kenntnisse und Fähigkeiten[3]:** z. B. Computerkenntnisse oder Fremdsprachen. Schreiben Sie, ob Sie nur Basiswissen haben, oder schon fortgeschritten sind.
- **Hobbys:** Schreiben Sie, was Sie in Ihrer Freizeit gerne machen. Sind Sie Mitglied eines Clubs oder einer Sportmannschaft? Schreiben Sie hier nicht zu viele Hobbys auf, sonst machen Sie den Eindruck, dass Sie für die Arbeit keine Zeit haben!

[1]übersichtlich *clear*
[2]Familienstand *marital status*
[3]Kenntnisse und Fähigkeiten *skills*

Presentation

First you have 10–15 minutes to look at the information below.
Then give a short presentation about the topic of taking part in sport. You should talk for 3–5 minutes.

Taking part in sport

What sports do people take part in?

Many people like to watch sports. But for many people the most interesting sports are the ones they can take part in[1], such as football, hockey, rugby, tennis and volleyball.
For some people, normal sports aren't exciting enough.
They like the danger and risk which come with "extreme" sports like rock climbing, bungee jumping, parachuting from planes or surfing where there are huge waves in the sea.

[1] to take part (in) *(an etwas) teilnehmen*

Why take part in sports?

European teenagers aged 16–19 who regularly take part in sports were asked: "Why do you do sport?"

This graph shows their answers.

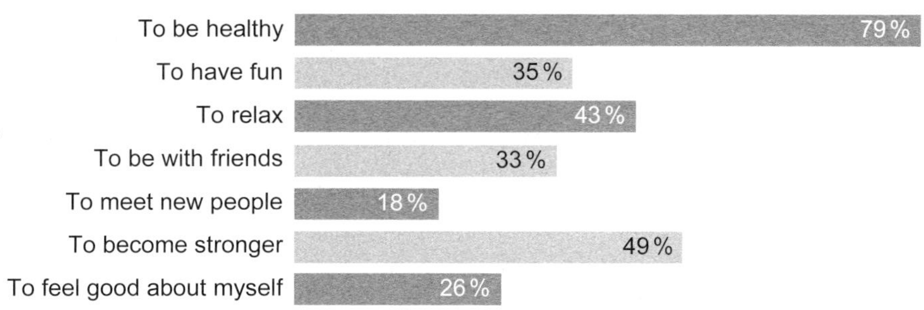

How much sport do European teenagers do?

It is different from country to country, between boys and girls, and at different ages. This graph shows how many teenagers in Germany and England do some sport *outside school* at three different ages: at 11 years old, at 13 years old, and at 15 years old.

— Who does more sport: boys or girls?
— Do teenagers do more or less sport when they get older?

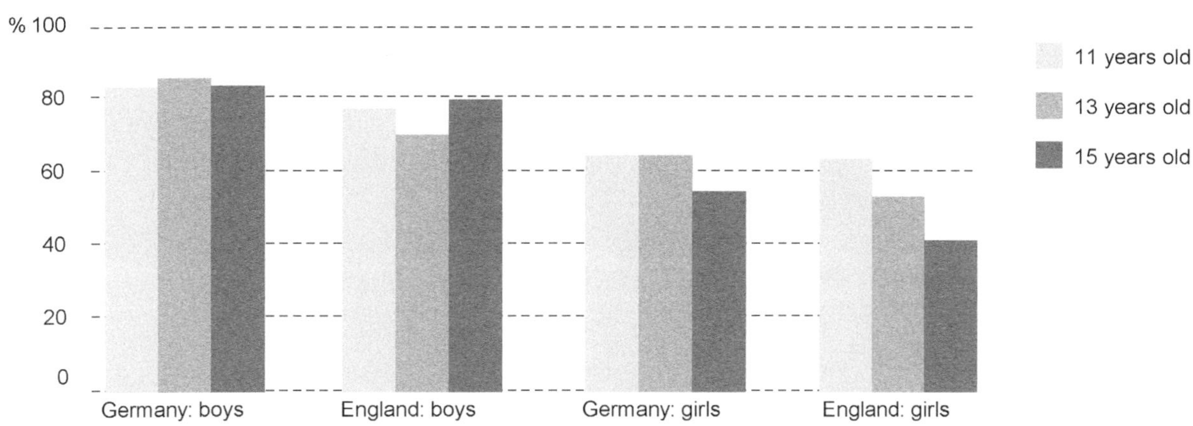

Do teenagers do enough sport?

Of course, doctors say "no". They say that teenagers everywhere in the USA and Europe should try to do more sport. One reason why teenagers are not fit enough, they say, is because they do other things which are not active, for example watching TV or listening to music.

Responding to visual prompts

Examiner: I'm going to give each of you a photograph. Candidate A, here is your photograph. Would you show it to Candidate B and talk about it for about one minute, please?

Candidate A

Examiner: Now Candidate B, here is your photograph. Would you show it to Candidate A and talk about it for about one minute, please?

Candidate B

Examiner: Thank you very much. Your photographs show people spending their free time outside. Now, I'd like you to talk together about the outdoor activities you like and the ones you don't like. Explain why and discuss your opinions.

H | PICTURE BANK: OVERVIEW

The pictures in the Picture Bank can be used to practise responding to visual prompts. They can be used individually or in pairs. Suggestions for use can be found in the introduction to Section B: *Responding to visual prompts*.

The topics of the pictures are:

1 Leaving home/travelling/hitchhiking (H1, H2)

2 Natural disasters (H3, H4)

3 Pets (H5, H6)

4 Working with animals / working with children (H7, H8)

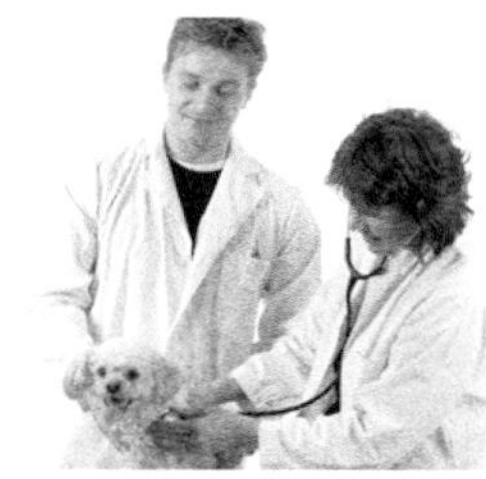
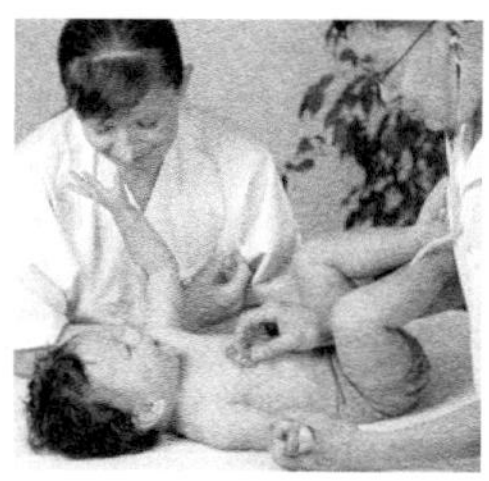

5 Hunger/overeating – food distribution throughout the world (H9, H10)

6 People quarrelling (H11, H12)

7 The supernatural (H13, H14)

8 Celebrations
(H15, H16, H17)

9 Unusual homes
(H18, H19)

10 Strange situations
(H13, H14, H20)

10 Saying 'No'
(H21)

11 Diet and exercise
(H22)

12 Modern technologies
(H23, H24, H25)

13 Modern technologies and the generation gap
(H24, H25)

KEY AND MODEL DIALOGUES

Note: Useful phrases are underlined.

E1.1

2 e / 3 f / 4 g / 5 b / 6 c / 7 a

E1.2

Hello, my name is Ted. Today I would like to talk about my favourite hobby – collecting stamps. First of all, I would like to tell you how I started this hobby. Then I'll show you some of the stamps I have brought with me today.

I started this hobby when I was eight years old, and my uncle gave me the stamp collection he had when he was a boy.

There are a lot of different ways of finding interesting stamps. Let me give you a couple of examples. One way is to have pen friends who live in other countries. I have two – one in Japan and one in Canada. Another way is to join a stamp collectors' club, either online or in the town where you live. You can also get stamps on e-bay.

If you get stamps on letters or parcels, you have to remove them. I would like to explain the best way to do that: put the stamp face down in warm water. Leave it for a few moments, and then it is easy to take it off the paper. Dry it with paper towels.

Now I would like to show you some of my best stamps. This one is from Japan. It's not very valuable, but it's very pretty, don't you agree? The next one is …

That was the last stamp I wanted to show you, and it brings me to the end of my presentation. Thank you for listening. And now I would be happy to answer any questions.

TEST ONE

General conversation

Sample dialogue

Yannick Hello, my name is Yannick. What's your name?

Michelle My name's Michelle. And my surname's Rosenbusch.

Yannick Can you spell that?

Michelle Yes, it's R-O-S-E-N-B-U-S-C-H. And what's your surname?

Yannick My surname is Orphanopoulos.

Michelle That's a difficult name. How do you spell it?

Yannick O-R-P… er, O-R-P-H-A-N-P… sorry … O-R-P-H-A-N-O-P-O-U-L-O-S.

Michelle Oh, I see. Are you Greek, Yannick?

Yannick Well, my dad was born in Greece and my mother is German. What about you, Michelle?

Michelle My parents are both from Kulmbach, but my grandparents came from Poland.

Yannick Oh, did they? Have you got any brothers or sisters?

Michelle Yes, I've got two sisters and a brother. My two sisters are a little older than me, but my brother is younger.

Yannick What are their names?

Michelle They're called Anna-Lisa, Franziska and Nico. And you? Have you got any brothers or sisters?

Yannick No, I'm an only child. But I've got lots of friends. Do you live in Kulmbach, Michelle?

Michelle Well, not really. We live in a little village called Hutschdorf. It's about 13 kilometres away from Kulmbach. I have to get up very early to get the school bus.

Yannick From our flat it's only 500 metres to school. It's great. By the way, what's your favourite school subject, Michelle?

Michelle Well, let me see … I like history and PE. But I don't like maths or physics.

Yannick Oh, really? That's interesting. My favourite subject is maths, but I'm not very keen on history. Actually, it's my worst subject. I can never remember the exact dates. How do you manage to remember all those details?

Michelle Well, I think it's because I like reading historical novels. I must have read over 50, I guess. That's why I already know a lot of the things our history teacher tells us. What kind of books do you like reading, Yannick?

Yannick Well, I'm a science fiction fan. I've read a lot of science fiction books and seen quite a few science fiction films. *Star Wars* is my favourite. Are you interested in science fiction?

Michelle Well, erm … I can't say science fiction is my thing. I've only seen the first *StarWars* film and I didn't like it very much. But Harrison Ford is a great actor. His best film is *The Fugitive*, I think. What do you think?

Yannick Yes, you're right. He's brilliant. My favourite Harrison Ford film is *Air Force One*. It's a great action film.

Michelle Yes, I know. It was on TV a few weeks ago.

Examiner Well, I think time is up. Thank you very much.

Role play

Sample dialogue

Mother Good morning, Sandy. How are you?

Daughter Okay.

Mother Did you sleep alright?

Daughter Yes, Mum.

Mother Sandy, could I ask you something?

Daughter What, Mum?

Mother Well, is everything okay? Is there anything you'd like to talk about?

Daughter Everything's okay, Mum. Why do you ask?

Mother It's just that you've been very quiet, and I wondered if there was anything wrong.

Daughter What should be wrong?

Mother Well, is everything okay with you and Sam?

Daughter Of course, Mum. We had an argument on Saturday. But I spoke to him yesterday and everything is alright. He says he still loves me.

Mother Do you believe him?

Daughter What do you mean, Mum? Listen, you have no right to ask me questions.

Mother But I'm your mother, and I worry about you.

Daughter You don't have to worry about me. I can take care of myself.

Mother It's just that ....

Daughter Look, would you mind just leaving me alone?

Mother Sandy, there's something I've got to tell you. I saw Sam in Meg's Café. He was with somebody.

Daughter Are you trying to tell me he was with another girl?

Mother Yes, I'm sorry.

Daughter Mum, I don't believe you. You've never liked Sam. You're just trying to come between us.

Mother Sandy, that's not true. I just want to help you.

Daughter I don't want your help. I'm going out. I'm going to meet Sam.

Mother Oh, dear ....

Mediation English-German

Lösungsvorschlag

- Schauen Sie sich die Wettervorhersage an, bevor Sie losfahren. Planen Sie eine Alternativroute, falls das Wetter schlechter ist, als erwartet.
- Ausrüstung, die man mitnehmen sollte: wasserdichte Kleidung, Wanderkarte, Kompass, Taschenlampe.
- Stellen Sie sicher, dass Sie die Route kennen und wissen, ob die Landschaft hügelig oder flach ist.
- Planen Sie die Wanderung und berücksichtigen Sie vor allem die Fähigkeiten der schwächsten Gruppenmitglieder.
- Nehmen Sie genug zu trinken und energiereiche Lebensmittel wie Schokolade, getrocknetes Obst und Nüsse mit. Warme Getränke oder Suppe können an kalten, nassen Tagen wohl tun.
- Es ist ratsam, regelmäßig kleine Mahlzeiten zu sich zu nehmen. Bonbons können einem helfen, den ganzen Tag Energie zu haben.
- Nehmen Sie immer Ihr Handy mit – am besten in einer wasserfesten Tasche. Im Notfall kann man dann sofort Hilfe rufen.

Simulated situation

Examiner I'm going to describe a situation to you. Your Aunt Betty, who is 53, is very lonely. That's why she wants to find a new spare time activity where she can get fit and meet other people. Decide which activity would be best for her, and talk about where in your area she could do it. Explain why you have chosen that activity, and discuss your opinions. Here is a picture with some ideas to help you. Just think for a few seconds. I'll say that again. Your Aunt Betty, who is 53, is very lonely. That's why she wants to find a new spare time activity where she can get fit and meet other people. Decide which activity would be best for her, and talk about where in your area she could do it. Explain why you have chosen that activity, and discuss your opinions. All right? Talk together.

Michelle Aunt Betty would like to find a new spare time activity. What do you think she should do?

Yannick Maybe she could go to a drama club. If you're a member of a club, you meet a lot of different people. The local drama club meets once a week. I think it's on Fridays. They meet in the old school building. What do you think?

Michelle That's a good idea. But she also wants to get fit at the same time. In a drama club you act in plays, but you don't get fit.

Yannick Oh, yes. I forgot that she wants to get fit, too. We'll have to think of something different then.

Michelle What about some excitement? There's a new bungee jumping club in town. They practise in the old factory. Aunt Betty would meet lots of interesting people there.

Yannick You must be kidding. Can you imagine Aunt Betty hanging on a rope? I think she's a bit too old for that kind of activity, isn't she? And I don't think she'd like it much.

Michelle Well, maybe you're right. If you ask me, Aunt Betty should go to a gym. I go to the one next to the church. If she goes there regularly, she'll be fit again in no time at all.

Yannick Do you really think so? I'm not so sure. I know that Aunt Betty likes eating very much. She's very fond of Italian food. Why don't we tell her to go on a cookery course? The evening school offers Italian cooking on Monday evenings. And the Italian cook is very charming. I saw his photo in the newspaper the other day.

Michelle That's a great idea! Maybe she could cook us some spaghetti or pizza after she's finished her course. But there's one problem. Remember that she also wants to get fit. Cooking meals won't make her any fitter. We'll have to think of something else.

Yannick How about karate? I don't think karate is as dangerous as bungee jumping. You can learn it at any age.

Michelle To tell you the truth, I don't think it's a good idea. The nearest karate club is 25 kilometres away from here. Aunt Betty wouldn't like driving that far every week.

Yannick Yes, you're right. Maybe the training would be too hard for her. And you can't talk very much when you practise because you have to concentrate.

Michelle What's your view on table tennis? In my opinion, that's the perfect activity for Aunt Betty. The club is only a hundred metres from her house. And the club members often do other activities together. There's a party every year. They also go on short weekend trips together. What do you think?

Yannick That's a really brilliant idea! Aunt Betty can play table tennis and get a little fitter. She'll get to know lots of other people, too. She can take part in the club's other activities if she wants to. Let's tell her to join the table tennis club then.

Michelle OK, yes. That's agreed then.

Examiner Thank you. That's the end of the test.

TEST TWO

General conversation

Sample dialogue – see TEST ONE

Mediation German-English

Lösungsvorschlag

Your CV must contain all important facts. It must be clear and easy to read. You can write your CV as a table. It can be arranged in the order of time ("chronological") or starting with the present situation ("American"). It must contain the following information:

Personal data: Your name, address, date and place of birth, and your marital status.

Education: If this is your first job, you can begin with primary school. You should mention your final school qualification and mark.

Work experience: Note all the jobs you have had so far and what you had to do. Describe practical training, part-time jobs or other activities.

Skills: For example, computer skills or foreign languages. Write down whether you have basic or advanced knowledge.

Memberships and hobbies: Write down what you like doing in your free time. Are you a member of a club or a sports team? Don't write down too many hobbies or you might give the impression that you have no time to work!

Presentation

Lösungsvorschlag

My name is Matthew and I'm going to talk about the topic: taking part in sport. My presentation is made up of four parts. First I'll describe some sports in general. Then I'll say why people take part in sports. After that I'll give some facts about how much sport teenagers in Europe do. And finally I'll answer the question: do teenagers do enough sport?

First, then, what are some of the sports that people take part in? There's a difference, of course, between spectator sports – the sports that people watch on TV, for example – and the sports which they take part in themselves. I'm talking only about taking part in sports. There are lots! In Europe, some of the most popular are football, hockey, tennis, basketball and volleyball. There is also a type of sport which people call 'extreme sport'. Two examples are bungee jumping and rock climbing. Some people like these sports because they enjoy risk and danger. Lots of people think extreme sports are pretty crazy, but the fans of extreme sports say they're great, and they have lots of skills, so that the sports aren't really so dangerous.

I'd like to go on now to the question: why do people take part in sports? Statistics for European teenagers show that there are different reasons, but the most important is clear. It's because people want to be healthy, and taking part in a sport is a healthy thing to do. Other reasons are: to make your body strong and fit, to have fun, and to be with friends.

Now I'd like to talk about how much sport European teenagers do. Almost all students do sport in school, so I'd like to look at people who do sport outside school. Generally speaking, we can say that in Germany, about 80 % of boys and 60 % of girls take part in a sport outside school. In England, it's about 75 % of boys and around 50 % of girls. Two points are really important. First, boys do more sports outside school than girls. And second, teenagers do less sport when they get older. A good example of this is girls in England. When they're 11 years old, over 60 % take part in some sport outside school. But when they're 13, it's 50 % and when they're 15, it's only 40 %.

Finally, I'd like to answer the question: do teenagers do enough sport? Doctors and other people say 'no'. The most important reason why teenagers aren't fit is that they do lots of other things that aren't active, for example watching TV, listening to music or sitting in front of the computer.

I'd like to finish by summarising the important points of my presentation. There are lots of different sports that people can take part in themselves. Some of these – they're called extreme sports – can be dangerous. People take part in sports for lots of reasons. The most important is to be healthy. Statistics say that boys take part in more sport outside school than girls, and that teenagers do less sport when they get older. Finally, doctors say teenagers don't do enough sport. They spend too much time doing things where they are not active.

That brings me to the end of my presentation. Are there any questions?

Responding to visual prompts

Examiner I'm going to give each of you a photograph. Candidate A, here is your photograph. Would you show it to Candidate B and talk about it for one minute, please?

Candidate A (Michelle) I think the photo was taken in a zoo or national park. It must be spring or summer because the people in the photo are wearing T-shirts and the sun is shining. In the foreground I can see two bears. One bear is standing and the other bear is sitting. There is a wall in front of the bears and some people behind it looking at the bears and taking photos of them. The wall goes from the bottom right to the top left of the picture. I'm not sure, but I think that there could be other animals there, and the wall is there to stop them escaping. The bears are looking at the people; perhaps they are hoping that they will give them some food. At the top of the picture there are lots of trees. I think the people are tourists who have come to the park to see the animals, and enjoy the sun.

Examiner Thank you very much. Now, Candidate B, here is your photograph. Would you show it to Candidate A and talk about it for about one minute, please?

Candidate B (Yannick) OK, thank you. I think my photo was taken on a school trip to the country. It must be autumn because there are leaves on the ground, but I don't think it's cold. In the foreground I can see a group of boys and none of them are wearing coats. They're all between 12 and 14 years old, I think. They're putting up a tent. One of the boys is just watching, and the other two are talking to each other, maybe about the best way to do it, but it looks like they've nearly finished. The boys are all wearing outdoor clothes; jeans, T-shirts and jumpers, and there's a rucksack on the ground. In the background I can see two other boys. They're sitting outside their tent. They've already put it up so now they seem to be relaxing.
I'm not sure, but I think they're probably from the same school. I think they're all having fun, and I'm pretty sure they're going to spend the night in their tents, maybe even the whole week.

Examiner Thank you very much. Your photographs show people spending their free time outside. Now, I'd like you to talk together about the outdoor activities you like and the ones you don't like. Explain why and discuss your opinions.

Yannick Well, let me think, … in winter I love skiing. We often go to Austria at the weekend. In summer I like swimming very much. If it's hot, I go swimming every afternoon. What about you, Michelle?

Michelle Hmm, swimming isn't my thing. But I like riding my bike in the afternoon. I got a brand new mountain bike for my birthday; it's great. I often meet my friends Julia and Christina after school, and we ride our bikes along the river. Have you got a bike, Yannick?

Yannick Yes, I have. But my bike is quite old. I only ride it to school sometimes. And sometimes my friends and I cycle to a little lake. We like lying in the sun after swimming, and listening to music. We usually play volleyball as well, and at the weekend we also often have barbecues near the lake. It's great fun.

Michelle Oh yes, I've heard. My friend Janna was there when you had a barbecue last month. She said it was great, but she didn't play volleyball.

Yannick Why don't you come, too? We're going there again next weekend.

Michelle Well, why not? At the weekend my parents always go on long walks in the countryside. They always want me to go with them, but I hate going on long walks, especially with my parents. It's awful.

Yannick I know what you mean. I hate visiting relatives in summer. My parents and our relatives sit in the garden for hours, and all they do is talk. It's so boring.

Michelle Oh, I see. Well, let's have a barbecue on Saturday then. We can go to the lake in the afternoon and have the barbecue in the evening. I can't stand playing volleyball, but I could bring my badminton rackets.

Yannick Badminton? I don't really like playing badminton very much, but we'll be in a big group so everybody can choose what they want to do. And I've got some new CDs. I'm absolutely crazy about the new *Coldplay* album. Why don't we listen to it in the evening?

Michelle Yes, OK. See you on Saturday then.

Examiner Thank you very much.